The Whipple Brunch: A Journey Through Cancer
the fears, tears, tiaras, & tornadoes

"My disbelief in miracles has been well shaken by the contents of this book. That a woman's insides can be removed, cleansed, detoxified, returned to the body, the cancer sliced away, and her body made whole again, is one great, superbly written, autobiographical epic. *The Whipple Brunch* by Andrea Tobin Cleghorn will leave you, mouth agape, laughing and filled with wonder. You will want to find her and hug this gloriously funny woman for going through this tunnel of death and emerging triumphant."

Malachy McCourt, *author,* A Monk Swimming

"We may think we did a perfect operation, but our job is not done until we take time to listen to the perspectives of our patients."

Carlos Fernandez del-Castillo, M.D.
Director, Pancreatic and Biliary Surgery, Massachusetts General Hospital

"In this beautiful and well-written memoir, literary raconteur Andrea Cleghorn delivers an unforgettable account of her serious medical experience. *The Whipple Brunch* never strays far from the reality of her subject matter; her words just make it lighter, more bearable and unexpectedly funnier than anyone has to date. This charming book carves out a unique place on the cancer memoir shelf. It is a real gem – can't wait for the film!"

Patty Ewald
former Executive Director, the Actors Studio

"For all cancers of all stages there will always be survivors. Andrea's journey supports keeping hope alive every day."

Francis J. McGovern, M.D.
Urological Oncological Surgery, Massachusetts General Hospital

"*The Whipple Brunch* is an amazing achievement: It's informative, funny, painful, engaging and impossible to put down. Wonderfully written, it gives the reader a frank look at an extreme surgical procedure, while at the same time underscores the value of courage, humor, friendships and, above all, hope. Andrea Cleghorn's uplifting story is one of the human spirit and the healing power of love."

Kathy McCoy, Ph.D.
author, The Teenage Body Book

The Whipple Brunch

Published by Ginkgo Books, Bedford, Massachusetts

No part of this book may be reproduced, scanned, or transmitted in any form
or by any means without permission in writing from the publisher, except
in the case of brief quotations embodied in critical articles or reviews, with
appropriate citation. Address correspondence to Permissions, Ginkgo Books,
87 South Road, Bedford, MA 01730.

Library of Congress Cataloging-in-Publication Data

LCCN: 2015917583

Cleghorn, Andrea

    The Whipple Brunch: A Journey Through Cancer / Andrea Cleghorn

        p. cm.

Books trade paperback ISBN 978-0-9969354-0-1

Illustrations by Embla Vigfusdottir

Interior Book design by Bill Michalski

Author photo by Susan Ellis

Cover Design by Anthony David Adams

Cover photo by Andrea Cleghorn

PRINTED IN THE UNITED STATES OF AMERICA

The Whipple Brunc

A Journey Through Cancer
the fears, tears, tiaras, & tornado

Andrea Cleghorn

Ginkgo Books
BEDFORD, MASSACHUSETTS

*Dedicated to the memory
of my mother, Katherine Coan Tobin,
and my father and namesake, Andrew Tobin,
who lived their lives with kindness, joy, and optimism.*

Table of Contents

Preface

Remember the time there was a tornado coming and we were afraid you would lose power?

No, Liz, I don't.

I drove to your house late one afternoon and when I got there I looked at the sky; it was this funny green color.

No.

Oh, yes, you do. You had the vacuum wound pump and we were trying to figure out how long it could run on battery. And Eileen stayed overnight so she could get you to the hospital if the pump shut down.

Nope.

I think that was the time Linda was racing over to your house and a tree fell across the road, missing her car by seconds...

Doesn't sound familiar. And I don't remember saying
I thought I was the Great Pumpkin, but I trust the
people around me when they say I did.

What I do remember is begging people to stop making
me laugh because it hurt my belly so much.

I didn't set out to write a book. But after the fourth
or fifth time someone said, "You can't make this stuff
up," I started keeping notes. Almost all of this book
was written in a prone position.

My medical care could not have been better, I remember that. I do not name the institutions, medical staff
– or institutions – to provide anonymity, since I did
not ask anyone's permission to write a book. I have
never encountered such caring, intelligent people and
it was easy to put my trust in them. I never considered I was battling cancer, as much as playing a part
of a powerful team effort to get me well.

At one point, my kidney surgeon said to me, "I know
you will do the right thing, you always do the right
thing." And this very comment made me want to do
the next right thing at those times when I got discouraged and wanted an easy way out.

My family kept in close touch primarily by phone and
email, since only one lives within a thousand miles
of me. My family of friends held and continue to hold
the memories for me: the painful times, the uncertain
times, and the crazy times. I know they were at times
much more worried than I was.

Just recently I was sitting in a restaurant with a bunch of my women friends and someone said to me, "Remember the time I drove you to the emergency room?"

Someone else said, "Oh, I did it once, too."

My friend Pat called out, "We *all* have. In fact, raise your hand if you've never driven Andrea to the emergency room! We refer to it as 'putting on the red cape.'"

They are superheroes, every one, and I am deeply, eternally grateful. Theirs were not random acts of kindness, like paying the toll for the car behind you on the Mass Turnpike. Their help was unrelenting, they provided backup when I didn't know I needed help, actively resisted it.

Even if I get things wrong, even if I don't remember details, I will never forget the village that took this child in.

Bedford, Massachusetts

1

Skellig Michael

Summer was over, students of all ages had returned
to school and I took off on my umpteenth trip to Ireland. Something about the Irish experience kept me
going back and back. Perhaps it was the landscape, or
the music, the pub life with the stories and the humor,
the *craic*, the people themselves.

What began with one week-long writing assignment
for a newspaper travel section in 2002 begat more,
and pretty soon I was traveling over there every
chance I got. There were many hilarious, unpredictable, adventure (read *mishap)*-filled weeks with my
friends. We stayed in houses we rented, borrowed
or swapped.

The Irish people felt like my tribe, and for good
reason; my grandparents had immigrated to Albany,

New York, from Counties Kildare and Kilkenny in the early 1900s. I became so enamored of Irish life that I plowed through a mountain of paperwork and obtained my own citizenship a century after John Patrick and Delia came to America.

Oh, yes, and for me there came to be the attraction of an anachronistic Irish gentleman I had met on a house swap in County Waterford. He was the neighbor who always seemed to be out trimming his hedge when we noisy Americans happened by with Sophie and Pinch, the dogs who came with the house belonging to the people who were currently staying at mine in Massachusetts.

Francis lived in a small cottage overlooking a pub on a tiny road, little more than a *boheen*, or lane, which dead-ended at a pier with a rocky beach on either side. The village hadn't changed much since pictures that were taken around 1900, and the pub had been there even longer.

Francis and I had few activities, but they included walking his wild Airedales up into the hills or along the two-mile sandbar every morning; eating wild game, fish, or beef with piles of snowy potatoes and drinking his own wine with dinner; sitting in wing chairs and drinking Irish porter by the fire, listening to music, playing the flute (for me, it had been decades) and even reading aloud. He was retired, and enjoyed puttering around the house during the day and staying very close to home.

He had traveled a bit in his early life, been to Greece, fought in Cypress and lived in London for several years, but never to the United States, and had no intention of getting on a plane again.

His dining room had the traditional Sacred Heart picture of Christ on the wall, an eternal red light always burning under it. I asked why he, a nonbeliever, would keep it there. He initially said it came with the house. He'd had the house forever, which made me wonder. Then he said it had saved his life when he was doing some rewiring and at one point was certain the power was out. At just the right moment, he noticed the light that proved him wrong. The red light stayed.

He was good company, literary and smart, and we definitely had good times, but at the same time there was a distinct darkness layered under the surface, a poignancy that was an almost universal part of the Irish heritage as well. I learned the legends, the superstitions, but also the Irish perspective on the past, from brutal treatment in school to living in the oppressive and violent time of the Troubles.

It seemed like time travel to an earlier century, and for the most part a way of life I had only read about.

And yet.

"You would be bored out of your knickers if you lived here," he told me early on.

He was right. I would drive to his house as soon as I landed in Dublin or Shannon, but after a few lovely days I was eager to get into a rental car, hit the left side of the road at 100 km an hour, and see what I could see in the rest of the country.

And, besides, I had a lofty goal. Some people dream of hiking the Appalachian Trail. I wanted to climb Skellig Michael, one of a pair of rugged islands across the country, about seven miles off the west coast of County Kerry.

Skellig Michael is a spiritual destination as well as an adventure. Monks lived there for centuries, possibly as early as 500 A. D., vacating a few centuries later. Theories abound about what happened, because it's Ireland, remember, but they built mortar-less beehive dwellings and a monastery named for St. Michael, a saint associated with high places such as Mont Saint-Michel in France. They also installed 600 steps to get up there from the wild water of the Atlantic.

The whole island is now a UNESCO site and attracts visitors from all over the world. I had wanted to go forever. To me, the Skelligs were compelling much the way whitewater rafting is appealing: It's exciting, requires little real skill, makes a big impression, and it's all over in a few hours.

I had seen the islands from afar. Michael is visible from many points along the coast, along with its baby sister, Little Skellig, shorter and fatter and covered with gannets. The pair make an incredible sight, at dawn, in the shifting light of day or just barely visible through the mist. "Skellig" comes from the Irish word for steep rock.

It might as well have been Everest. To me, it was climbing a mountain and swimming the English Channel and running a full marathon all tied up in one. Terrified of heights, with little faith in my own agility, I seldom take risks in the physical realm. But I was as ready as I would ever be, and in preparation had been going to the gym regularly for, well, a while.

The first hurdle in getting to the Skelligs has always meant finding a day that boats will attempt the passage. Thirteen vessels assess conditions every morning. There is no such thing as a smooth ride to Skellig Michael, even on the calmest of days. On the iffy days, the captains get a consensus and either all the boats go out or none.

This particular year my friend Eileen came with me. It wasn't her dream destination, but she was – and is – a good sport. I had tried several years to get to Skellig Michael but the boats weren't running.

This one turned out to be the lucky day, following a week of no-go. We climbed aboard. The ride would take "somewhere from 45 minutes to two hours." I tried to picture making the trip in a *curragh*, the traditional wooden frame vessel covered with animal skins.

This was a good day, but even so, the voyage was so choppy we had to hold on tight to avoid flying into the chilly waters. A miracle over-the-counter medication called Sealegs ensured getting over and back in one piece. The crossing from Port Magee, south of Valencia in County Kerry, was as rocky as the destination.

When we landed, I took a look at the climb ahead of me. Not so bad, I thought. And how hard can it be to climb a few hundred stairs? I climb 13 every night when I go to bed and have done that hundreds, maybe thousands of times. But the stairs in a house usually stay more or less put when you step on them.

Eileen urged me on, and said she would catch up, walking at her own pace. Anyway, I set out and up.

Some parts are steep, many are on the side of a cliff, and labeling these structures "steps" is a compliment. They are as wide as stairs but made of multiple shifting pebbly chunks of crumbling stone. Some require giant leaps, others, minor hops.

Fair to say they were roughly horizontal. I got up them, but didn't exactly scamper. I checked and double-checked my footing. Luckily it was a dry day. If they had been slippery, there is no doubt in my mind someone would have slid into the Atlantic, and it probably would have been me.

The other notable thing about Skellig Michael concerned handrails. No handrails. There was only one set of stairs, so if someone was coming down while you were going up. Ooh. It's much like driving in Ireland, but without the collision damage waiver on the insurance.

Christ's Saddle, a wide, flattish area partway up, provided a reprieve, a somewhat level place to rest, take a drink or retrieve a bite of food (you thought to bring along) before continuing.

But I got to the top and, once there, Eileen wasn't far behind me. I was delighted to make it at all, avoiding the one thing that would have ruined the day: falling off. Two Americans were not so lucky just the previous year.

The view from the monastic settlement was truly awesome, colorful, and not too scary, even at something like 600 feet. We could see the Atlantic Ocean all around us, the West of Ireland coastline, and many islands. Those monks had put up a shoulder-high rock wall, handy for leaning against for selfies with Little Skellig in the background. Surprisingly, the area was crowded with people at the top.

A small cemetery, chock-a-block with crosses, shared space with remnants of a garden. There was little if any soil really, so the dozen monks did what the Irish have done for all of history. They put together lazy beds – seaweed and sand to provide a base for growing vegetables. The ground may have been lazy, but certainly not the men who fed themselves from what they could grow in this mostly cold, windy, inhospitable place. The monks fished, of course, and captured birds and the eggs left behind.

There was one intact typical dwelling structure where three monks could sleep, with cupboards made of stone and pegs – also stone – to hang their belongings.

I never saw the historic monastic latrine mentioned in the UNESCO literature, strategically constructed over a deep ravine. Maybe that was on the path up to South Peak, now closed, which had been accessible only through a crevasse in the rocks called the Needle's Eye, as wide as a human foot.

We had more than an hour up there before we needed to go down those same steps, which proved a little less strenuous but even more daunting because of the difficulty in maintaining balance.

The crossing back over the water was much smoother, though, a quick trip.

A few days later I flew home from Ireland in good spirits, with a notebook full of stories, a year's worth of potatoes and Smithwicks lager under my belt, and a camera card showing roadways lined with the flame-colored wildflowers called Montbretia, checkerboard green fields, and red-haired people.

I felt great, lucky to have gone to Ireland once again. I was proud to achieve this little goal, content to return home and pick up my ordinary life at the time of the year when Massachusetts is at its best, brilliant in golds and oranges and reds.

I had no idea that two weeks later the bottom would drop out from under me, radically changing my expectations and any plans I might have had.

Life would not be ordinary for a very long time.

2

It begins: A twinge, then a jackhammer

The phone rang one quiet Friday night. It was Suzy, one of my friends from way, way back. She and I had been in the freshman dorm at the University of Kansas. We were mainly Christmas card friends at this point, but whenever we did talk, she was as much fun as she was when we were 18. This conversation was no exception.

After a little greeting, Suzy cut to the chase: She was following up on a reunion invitation she had sent to me early in the summer.

"When is it?" I asked.

I had a dim recollection of an email about a get-together in Kansas City. Suzy filled me in. It was a reunion of our close friends from Three South Corbin Hall, a freshmen girls' dorm.

College life in the freewheeling '60s hadn't held my attention for long – I was out of there after three semesters – but dorm life was the nuts. Freshman year in Corbin: If there was a wacky idea to try out, a skit, an outlandish prank, you can bet I was in on it.

Growing up, I wasn't allowed to watch much TV on school nights; my parents, both English majors in college, went over my themes until I was bleary-eyed. But no more. We were Girls Gone Wild 1966/67 version, which meant smoking cigarettes, sneaking beer into our rooms and hitchhiking all over town, though always wearing a stitched-down pleated skirt with a twin sweater set to class.

But back to my 21st century living room. When was it again? Oh, *this* weekend? The initial gathering had been at her house in Kansas City that very night.

As we talked, she told me this reunion needed some adrenaline.

"I made a DVD of music from the '60s," she said. "I thought we'd be bumping and grinding the night away – and then everyone left by 9:30."

That's when she decided she'd call me to talk me into coming. Bear in mind that I had never gone to a single reunion of any kind from any school I attended. This one was 1500 miles away, and I would need to fly out the next morning. (Got to love Google maps. It said I could walk there in 19 days and three hours. Oops, wrong button.)

Still, I have always had great memories of that year on Three South, and when Suzy called that night to talk about coming, it sounded as if it had possibilities. But was she serious? Was *I*?

How could I justify the extravagance of buying a plane ticket and taking off so soon when I was still unpacking from Shannon Airport? I had family members clamoring for my attention and a dog who was still following me room-to-room in the cautious euphoria of my return.

I got on the Internet to check prices. They were really very cheap, and there would be no other expenses. And I would be back in just a couple of days.

Still, there was yet another obstacle to this last-minute trip. I had invited about 25 people over for a potluck supper the following night. It would be a little cheesy to cancel out on that, but I had gatherings of the clan all the time, so would anyone really care?

About an hour into the phone conversation, though, I began to have a little twinge in my right side. I was seated in my most comfortable overstuffed chair in the living room, but I began to feel more and more uncomfortable.

Then the twinge became an ache. I changed position, twisting in the chair, but it didn't help. At one point I actually slid off the chair onto the rug. The ache was becoming a cramp. I took the phone upstairs and got a heating pad. It was becoming hard to laugh, then even talk.

I had to interrupt this telephone fun fest to tell Suzy that I just wasn't feeling good all of a sudden. I told her I'd check on the flights and call her from the airport in the morning if she needed to pick me up. That's how we left it.

Breathing was becoming difficult. Pretty soon I was in agony. The cramp had been replaced by a screwdriver, then a jackhammer aimed at my right side and going full blast.

I got back to the computer, took Kayak off the screen and got onto WebMD, where I self-diagnosed this new bizarre pain. What was worse than childbirth? A kidney stone, right. I honestly didn't remember childbirth as being a whole lot worse than this. I thought it was the wrong location for appendicitis (it actually could have been), so I was going with the kidney stone theory.

It was about 1 in the morning by this time. I woke up my son, who was sleeping upstairs. I told him I was in horrible pain, hardly getting the words out.

"Do you want to go to the hospital," he asked. No, of course not. So why did I wake him up? Because I was scared to be alone with it.

Within a very few minutes, I was begging him to drive me to the community hospital in the neighboring town. I didn't really consider an ambulance; I guess I considered that overreacting.

So off we went. It should have taken about 20 minutes, but of course there were no traffic worries. It was the fastest trip ever.

When we got to the emergency department, I got prompt attention. That in itself was a bad sign.

I was given painkillers immediately. Nothing touched it. I wanted to be knocked out.

After scans and blood tests and what seemed like 16 hours, the ER doc told me I had a hematoma in my kidney that had erupted and was pumping blood into my abdomen. He seemed sympathetic and worried. His attitude was almost as disturbing as hearing the words "erupted," "pumping," and "blood" in the same sentence.

The doctor left me in the curtained cubicle. When he returned, he said, "I'm afraid you're going downtown."

Uh-oh.

The doctor said he was sending me downtown.

Now, these are words that are feared by patients and criminals alike. When things go south medically almost anywhere in New England, downtown Boston is the place to be. I had already had kidney cancer surgeries twice, and felt lucky to be living where I did.

Ironically enough, when I was working at a newspaper downtown, my desk had a clear view of the medivac helicopters landing on a nearby rooftop. Technicians invariably jumped out with small beer coolers jokingly known as "kidney carriers."

Now I would get the ambulance ride I had rejected earlier. The community hospital, the Little Hospital, had a good reputation, but there was so much bleeding and I was being offered a lift to one of the best hospitals in the country.

I was scared enough to be glad to be going. Actually it wasn't exactly an offer. I was being kicked out because it was serious. I was given my choice of Boston hospitals, and it looked as if I could get a bed in the one I knew. I was relieved. Well, so much for the Three South Reunion.

Death seemed to be an acceptable Plan B.

I asked my son to wait in the quiet room next to the ER until he knew for sure what hospital I was going to.

Whatever medication was in my IV was finally starting to take hold, and I didn't know what to do so I let go. I would go where they wanted to send me, favorite downtown hospital or anyplace else. My 90-year-old mother was taken care of in assisted living, my daughter lived in California and I didn't want to worry her (yet). There would be no flying off to the Midwest or a potluck supper in my dining room.

I dozed off and was barely aware when I was transferred into the ambulance heading into town. In spite of the sirens, I fell into a dead sleep. I woke up when we got to Cambridge.

We went over the Charles River to Storrow Drive to Boston. The little slice of sky I could see was beginning to lighten.

3

Cambridge House, where the sick rich go

The ambulance seemed to be flying east on that early, early Saturday morning in October. We were headed to a place that was legendary in the minds of those in Boston and worldwide.

The Big Hospital was short on beds when I arrived, but that is how I won the lottery. To be assigned to the palatial Cambridge House was a stroke of good luck. How many hospital units get the designation "house"?

If a sitting president had been admitted, that would have been his or her room. Or a rock star. Or any old billionaire who hired a boutique doctor and expected the best. Mahogany paneling, fancy signage and great futons for sleepover guests created quite the ambience. Throw in a million-dollar view of Boston, the

Charles River and beyond to Cambridge. I thought "nice," and fell asleep. As it was, I could just barely appreciate my surroundings once daylight concluded that awful night.

In the morning light, the 46th annual Head of the Charles Regatta kicked off, with gusty winds and 40-degree temperatures. The chill had no effect on me, but brilliant sunshine with a bright blue sky was much appreciated. There would be literally thousands of rowers navigating the winding 3-mile course along the Charles River. It was a silent tableau; I could catch just a glimpse as I raised my head from the pillow.

Twelve years before, I had been in the Big Hospital for the treatment of renal cell carcinoma. At that time, I had a 2.5-pound tumor on my left kidney. Despite the size of the tumor, it was only discovered by an ultrasound for a relatively mundane gynecological problem. The kidney and tumor were removed.

Three years of uneventful follow-up scans later, a tiny tumor was detected and my left adrenal gland was surgically removed. Since then, I had been cancer-free for nine years. I knew I could get along fine with just one kidney.

Actually, I had lost one other organ. The year before the first kidney cancer episode, I had had my thyroid "put to rest," a euphemism for killing it with radioactive iodine. Graves disease, hyperthyroidism, was the reason for that, and simple thyroid replacement had made it part of my daily routine. I had lots of company with the Graves, including George and Barbara Bush and even Millie, their Springer Spaniel.

Still, I considered myself an extremely healthy person; I almost never got the flu or even caught cold.

When the ambulance delivered me to the Big Hospital that Saturday morning I was heavily medicated; I was literally feeling no pain. I was in a surreal state. I think it would be a year later that I remembered I had never called Suzy back about the reunion. Someone canceled the party I had scheduled for that night. Only one or two people showed up to an empty house, apparently.

Some of the guests ended up in my room at Cambridge House that day. The first morning turned out to be a sort of impromptu hospital shower and I got the loot.

One person brought a memory foam mattress and matching pillows to ease the pain of the hospital bed. The scowling nurse on duty said it was "flame-able" and absolutely not allowed. That's when I learned to wait for shift change and, sure enough, the next nurse was totally cool with it. It's a variation on the idea that if mom says no, ask grandma.

Nancy brought a camel-colored, soft-as-a-cloud throw lined with sheepskin. I have never fallen in love as hard as I fell in love for that blanket. Later, it had the added benefit of matching my dog's shedding hair.

People brought flowers, things to read, and, best of all, themselves. Some brought food. I wasn't allowed to eat anything that week and I didn't care. I learned they call it the Big Hospital diet. For the first time in my life food was totally unappealing to me.

Visitors told me the cafeteria food in the Big Hospital is fantastic ("the best omelet in the city of Boston"), and I really wouldn't know about patient food. I had no appetite, so it was just as well I was getting nutrition through the IV.

The nurses and aides at Cambridge House that weekend were exceptionally nice, with one screaming exception. As sick as I was, I really couldn't stand a certain nurse, the crabby, "flame-able" one. The hospital shower gifts were great, but I had no interest in the other kind, in which you are scrubbed down by someone you don't know and who doesn't really approve of what she sees. I told her I wouldn't do it.

"You have to, Stinky."

I took exception to the name-calling, although she was probably right. I was just too tired and shaky to move. There was no way to avoid it forever, though, and she got me into the stall, hovering because I was a fall risk, she fully clothed and me fully not. She was pretty stinky herself, reeking of garlic and rancid fried food. I thought, choking, well it takes one to know one.

Not much happened those first two days. It was the weekend, and that is typical, but I couldn't quite understand what was going on, even what people were telling me. Maybe it was some kind of self-protective fog. But I knew it just didn't sound good. Not good at all. Would the third round of kidney cancer be as straightforward as the first two, if that is what it even was?

After a slow weekend, the pace picked up.

My daughter called me from San Francisco and said she was on her way to Boston, no arguments please. I know she was scared; I was so glad to see her though, so appreciated the effort in leaving her job to spend the week with me.

I saw my kidney oncologist who had been following me for periodic cancer scans for all that time. When I met with him this time around he explained that because I was a longtime patient he had seen me as a courtesy all that time, but his specialty was testicular cancer now, and, frankly, I didn't have the right stuff. He referred me to another oncologist who would be a better fit. I was seeing him only every 18 months at that point, so I was fine with changing physicians.

I would be seeing my kidney surgeon from before, so that was reassuring to me.

The week was jam-packed with diagnostic tests, scans and exams. Blood draws and various IV requests came every few hours. I've never seen so many students crowded around one bed.

On Monday, there was angiography on a selective particulate embolization (blood clot) of the lower pole of the kidney. They needed to stop the bleeding from the mass on the right kidney. Results of the biopsy, which they referred to as "brushing," would be back in seven days. They assumed cancer, but the confirmation would come the following week.

On Tuesday physicians performed an ERCP (endoscopic retrograde cholangiopancreatogram – no wonder there was an acronym), using endoscopy and fluoroscopy for a better look, and inserted a stent in the common biliary duct to open up an obstruction in the liver. There was a wait for results on that, too.

From my perspective, it seemed the massive push for diagnosis wasn't resulting in a start of treatment anytime soon. "We have to wait for the blood to clear," I was told. The blood to the liver was cut off so it couldn't cause more damage, but it was questionable how much destruction had already been done.

The rest of the week was busy but also hazy. I would ask for translations after I was told something. A friend said several times when we were talking she thought I was thinking but I would actually be drifting off to sleep.

I soon knew there was a tumor, almost definitely malignant, on my kidney. It wasn't just the kidney, though. The common bile duct, the pancreas and I didn't know what other sites might be involved.

There were and would be lots of physicians making drawings for me on sheets of paper.

Because of the tremendous amount of blood that had gone into my abdominal cavity from the hemorrhage in the kidney, the doctors would have to wait until it was reabsorbed to decide what to do.

Circumstances facilitated the first step in surrendering. I understood I had to wait, I trusted they were doing all they could. Knowing and having confidence in my kidney surgeon from the first two episodes was a major benefit. They had to wait for biopsies and other test results to come in and, to a certain extent, for my body's ability to heal itself.

Still, from what I was taking in, this wasn't shaping up at all like the other cancer experiences. The tests came and went, I tried to be a cooperative patient. "Patient" was the operative word.

It would be the beginning of an experience that I never could have anticipated, the feeling of being cared for almost as a child by people I trusted and others I needed to choose to trust. And it was a choice.

There were some light moments, if you can call an inexplicable 30-pound weight gain humorous. When I got to the point that I was encouraged to get up and walk, my friend Eileen and I headed for the scale in the hall. We had already seen the bed scale reading and it was 10 pounds over my normal weight after a week of eating nothing. I got to the scale in the hall and it showed I was even 10 pounds heavier than the bed scale reading. So we found another scale and it was up another 10 pounds. Was this some kind of cosmic joke? After another few days of no food, would I be 400 pounds and need to be lifted out of my room with a crane?

My actual weight would be one of many absurd, even inexplicable, aspects of my hospital stay.

I was off and on one with the universe. I had kidney cancer again, but with the help of strong medicine I slept between tests, explanations. Actually, I often slept *during* explanations.

I kept reminding myself I had done beautifully the first two times. I had felt fine for the past nine years.

Renal cancer typically does not respond to chemo and radiation, so I assumed that when the inevitable surgery was over I would begin to recover.

This time around though, I only had one kidney.

4

Everybody's got an opinion

After a week of tests and procedures I'd never heard of, my daughter drove me home from the hospital. She needed to go back to her life in Berkeley and I needed to recover, to absorb this new development, much as my body was repairing itself after the massive internal bleeding from the kidney.

I didn't feel good at that point, in fact, I got sick to my stomach on the way home. But I wasn't in terrible pain, either. I was primarily just anxious and exhausted.

In the following weeks, the scans were updated several times and there was extensive testing of all kinds. Unfortunately, since my whole abdominal cavity had filled with blood, it was a waiting game for a while.

Finally all the test results were in. Apparently the hemorrhage in my kidney had done a lot of damage. I had a stent in the common bile duct, which would need to be replaced every three months or so. I was freaked out at the news. I would have to go to the hospital *every three months*? In hindsight, what a joke.

I finally had definitive confirmation of kidney cancer in both the lower pole of my right kidney and, as of early November, the head of my pancreas. This was in addition to the wreckage of my internal plumbing system. Kidney cancer has a reputation for being slow-growing but can metastasize along an unpredictable path, as mine had.

As I feared, though, it was a big, big deal.

The idea of having untreated cancer was making me a little crazy. I couldn't be Zen about it. I wanted to *do* something, or at least *make somebody do something*.

But I was all over the place, meditating, praying, talking to people, looking things up on the Internet.

At one point, I had thought I might actually do nothing at all. This was my third time around with kidney cancer. What were my chances? That attitude didn't last long; I quickly discarded the notion of no treatment. If I couldn't stand waiting to see how a protocol was working, how would it be to blow off every option I was offered and just see how long I could last? No, going along and ignoring it altogether didn't make any sense. Maybe if I had been 102 instead of 62.

After the first of the year, I went to my newly-assigned oncologist at the Big Hospital. He recom-

mended Sutent, a targeted treatment. Instead of
attacking all my cells, as chemo would do, it would hit
only the cancerous cells. It wouldn't cure the cancer,
but it would, at best, slow it down. There would be
side effects, though the degree of severity couldn't
be predicted.

Renal cell cancer was still considered resistant to both
chemotherapy and radiation, so those treatments
were not offered to me, the same as the last two times.
Surgery was the only option in my previous episodes.

Long ago I realized the importance of taking someone with me to medical appointments. It didn't have
to be a family member, just someone I trusted and
was concerned for my well-being. A companion could
listen with me, often for me, when my mind inevitably
started racing off in other directions.

Several years before, one of my good friends had
received a cancer diagnosis, and I could listen and
take notes while the information went flying right
over her head. She sat next to me and knit up a storm.
Years before, I recalled how my mother couldn't take
in a word the doctor said immediately after my dad
had a major stroke.

Just to cover bases, I tried to take two people with
me to appointments. Ideally, one of the friends would
have medical expertise, and the other needed only be
a good listener and asker of questions.

The other choice was something called a Whipple. I
had never heard of a Whipple procedure, but now I
know that is because I didn't see "Grey's Anatomy"
in Season 1. (Cristina pushed for the most aggressive

surgical treatment for her patient, who incidentally died of pancreatic cancer in a bed at Seattle Grace Hospital before she had the surgery.)

In real life, Allen Whipple developed the pancreaticoduodenectomy, now known as the Whipple, in the 1930s as a two-step procedure, which was later merged into one operation. It is primarily used to treat pancreatic cancer.

The Whipple procedure is also considered for other types of cancer that end up in the pancreas, as my kidney cancer had. It isn't the right course of action even for pancreatic cancer, though as only 10 to 15 percent of patients can benefit from it, for one reason or another.

It is a complicated surgery and involves removing the head of the pancreas (where my tumor was, the large end), as well as the distal artery of the bile duct, the gallbladder, part of the stomach, and the duodenum, which is a section of the small intestine. Then the pancreas, stomach and bile duct are sutured back onto the small intestine which has been stretched to reach those organs.

It essentially reroutes the entire digestive system.

In the first few decades of use, the Whipple was extremely risky. One in four patients didn't survive. Today, the odds are much, much better, but correlating to the expertise and experience of the pancreatic surgeon. No patient would want to be the first or second in a surgeon's career.

My oncologist wasn't advocating the Whipple. In fact, the way he presented it I didn't even think he considered it a serious option, and when he described it for the first time, my reaction was, "well, hell no."

His recommended option: the targeted treatment, "try it and wait and see." The other, his distant second choice, was the Whipple. It sounded like a bad joke.

I went home and called my insurance company to see if they would cover a second opinion; they would. In the end, I would talk to nine physicians. It was complicated, because the kidney cancer was in two different organs, so treatment was under the purview of two different specialists. And I needed to talk with both oncologists and surgeons.

If there was anything simple about this time after the diagnosis, it was obtaining second opinions. They were easy to arrange and schedule. Absolutely everyone in the medical establishment seemed to think they were a matter of course.

Had I expected histrionics, my own physician jumping on the desk and shouting, "WHAT! You don't trust me?" What I got instead was matter-of-fact efficiency.

On the other side, would the doctor want to know why I was wasting his/her time to check up on the doctor I was supposed to trust?

Wait a minute. Both these scenarios were out of a couple of generations ago, when Marcus Welby was practicing medicine...on black-and-white TV. Now we have the Internet and know everything, no medical school involved. It also means we get a choice, but sometimes wonder if we have the experience to make a good decision.

At any rate, on to the second hospital.

Off I went, taking two friends with me, one a doctor and the other a writer at a medical journal. I had gotten names of an oncologist, a kidney surgeon and a pancreatic surgeon. They all advocated Interleukin 2, which had been in the clinical study stage when I first had cancer and had my left kidney and its 2.5-pound tumor removed.

(I was offered to take part in the study at the time the cancer metastasized to the adrenal gland. The side effects for the study were daunting. At that time I had consulted with a friend, the medical director of a large cancer research institute. She listened to what I thought, and told me "This has one of the worst black box warnings I've ever seen." Yikes. I didn't do it.)

This time around the surgeon at the hospital I had chosen for a second-opinion said she would not recommend surgery.

"What is the point? Do you want to subject yourself to two surgeries, recover in between them? The cancer... is...in...your...*bloodstream*," said the doctor who wanted to make sure I knew what I was getting into.

She was essentially telling me I should think about whether I wanted to spend the precious time I had having one surgery after another, especially electing to have the Whipple which comes with a long recovery and frequent complications. Her comment scared the holy hell out of me. The other doctor there was also advising Interleukin 2.

I could feel myself tearing up; out-and-out crying soon followed. I couldn't stop; this was beginning to feel hopeless. No one in the room seemed to notice, not my two friends, not the doctors. I felt very alone and scared.

I had been to two hospitals now. The side effects of both drugs were serious, as far as I could tell, not just nuisance factors. Some patients in the trial had died, others couldn't tolerate their skin peeling off in sheets, the high fevers, the hospitalizations to administer the treatment. And the benefits didn't seem to warrant the risk.

Patients could get better with these treatments, but it wasn't a clear cure.

I was miserable. I didn't like either option.

Being new at the second opinion game, I was suspicious about taking a recommendation on a doctor from anyone who might have a vested interest. But I definitely wanted an opinion from a third medical institution, and that would be a cancer center.

I went to the website of the respected cancer research center in Boston and checked the list of kidney cancer oncologists. Most of the oncologists specialized in testicular and prostate cancer.

But there was an oncologist at the cancer institute who was just listed simply as treating kidney cancer, pure and simple. It was a woman's name, a rarity in that department.

I called and made an appointment with her. The scheduler also got appointments with a kidney surgeon and a pancreas surgeon for the same day. Here again, it was easy to get appointments, and also fast.

"They try to see people within 10 days," she told me.

My friend Linda, a retired nurse as well as my health care proxy, went with me to the cancer institute that day. It was just the two of us. We were shown into the oncologist's office, and before she appeared, an attending physician came in. He had a forgettable, unpronounceable name and an unforgettably engaging manner. If he was there to warm us up, it was working.

He asked me about my situation, although he seemed to already have information. His grasp of my situation was impressive. He listened, and then he said something that surprised me.

"Are you considering the Whipple?" he asked.

"Do you think it's really a feasible option?" I asked, frankly flabbergasted. Who would go along with that barbaric choice?

"I do. I think it's the way to go in a lot of cases. You're lucky you have kidney cancer because though it's unpredictable, it's also slow-growing. But, yeah, I would consider it."

The oncologist came in. I was a little surprised when *she* turned out to be a *he*, despite the first name I associated with people who happened to be women. We exchanged a little small talk, he talked about what he had seen in my scans and in the records. Then he stared into my eyes.

"What is the goal of cancer treatment?"

Trick question. I drew a blank.

"I don't know," I said.

"To cure you," he said. "Surgery is the answer, my final answer." There was an ominous tone in his voice.

I looked at Linda and she looked back at me. Neither of the two treatments would cure me. This was extreme, but would eliminate the cancer (and the suspense). It was the only option that would throw the cancer out. If the stats made any sense at all, if I honestly believed I could survive it, maybe this was what I wanted.

It made me think of a combination lock that hesitates just prior to the final number...then clicks into place. I knew what Linda was thinking and she knew what I was thinking.

"That's it." I knew it, she knew it. Suddenly, it made sense. I didn't want to buy myself some time; what if I felt lousy? I didn't want to chance the horrendous side effects of the non-surgical treatments.

Was I really going to do it? I think I was.

Before Surgery

Bile duct
Stomach
Gallbladder
Body and tail of pancreas
Head of pancreas
Duodenum
Small intestine

After Surgery

Bile duct attached to small intestine
Remaining pancreas attached to small intestine
Stomach attached to small intestine
Small intestine

I met with the kidney surgeon there who seemed very knowledgeable and was good about answering my questions, but was quite young and had done just 100 kidney cancer surgeries. I was hoping for more experience.

The other one, the pancreatic surgeon, had a lot of experience. They were colleagues at the same hospital, but the two surgeons had never met.

The pancreatic surgeon said, somewhat impatiently, I thought, "I don't know why you would hesitate on the surgery. If you don't have it, you'll be dead in a couple of years."

Thud.

I really didn't appreciate that comment, even though he was reiterating what I had heard earlier. Was it that I didn't like the messenger, a very tall man who towered over me as I sat and he stood? I felt sad, stupid, annoyed, vulnerable, even bullied. I wanted to go home and get under the covers.

My euphoric relief at making a decision had drained away. But before Linda and I left, I asked the two surgeons if it would be possible to do both operations at the same time to save myself recovering in between. They had never done that, but they both said they would consider it. It could work.

To save time later, would I sign a surgery consent form? No obligation. I did, even though it seemed premature, considering I had gone in that day totally opposed to having the Whipple at all. But that didn't mean I necessarily wanted to have it performed in their hospital. My brain wasn't capable of going through every option all at once. I was a little overwhelmed and wanted to get out of there; I signed the consent form.

If I had to have the surgery, and it seemed the only way to go, I wanted to go home. And home, in this case, was my original hospital, the Big Hospital with the kidney surgeon I liked, respected, and trusted.

Finally, I got home that afternoon, to the actual house where I lived. I remember taking to my bed immediately. I got up the next morning and went to work on it. After a very short time, probably within a few days, I had done a lot of research.

I was ready to pursue the Whipple route; it just seemed to make sense.

The facts rotated through my mind. The scary reputation was tied to looking at the diagrams, and I must admit watching the procedure on YouTube. The mortality rate of 25 percent was 50 years ago. If the pancreatic surgeon had a lot of experience – and a record of good outcomes – the risk would be minimized to a very low, statistically safe level.

Seattle Grace Hospital was definitely out of the running, and not because they only did a mere two Whipples a year. The larger problem was that the surgeons were television actors.

I talked with a couple of people who had had the procedure. It was still a bold move, but I decided it was the right one for me. Not everyone had the same experience.

I was told I could end up on dialysis ("think of it as a part-time job") spending three days a week getting my blood exchanged. I knew I could be diabetic; compared to cancer, it seemed a small price.

I needed to see if my kidney surgeon who had treated me twice would be available and agreeable to perform the kidney surgery. Then I needed to find a good pancreatic surgeon at the same Big Hospital. Those were big "ifs." But the best scenario would be that I could locate a pancreatic surgeon with a track record with many, many successful Whipples before my pancreas came on the OR scene. Did I say many?

At that point I didn't even know that in some cases the pancreatic surgeon doesn't recommend the Whipple for an individual patient. But if everything lined up just right, I would go for the Whipple at my home hospital.

Please let this be resolved soon, I thought, because I was getting queasy thinking about those unseen malevolent invaders.

5

Waiting for Whipple

I made appointments to see both a kidney surgeon and a pancreatic surgeon at the Big Hospital in Boston, the one I considered my home hospital. Until I had made the decision to go with the Whipple, I didn't need a surgeon. Now I had to have two, one for each cancer site.

My first choice for a kidney surgeon was a no-brainer. The same doctor had removed my left kidney 12 years before and my left adrenal gland when the kidney cancer metastasized to that organ three years later.

I met with Dr. Kidney, who was just as warm and professional as before. He had an Irish name, an Irish face, and he was as charming as he was professional. I had heard nothing short of raves about him as a doctor and a person. Totally reassuring.

"Written any books lately," he inquired. He not only remembered me, he remembered I had written a book about Rosie's Place, a women's homeless shelter in Boston, just prior to the first kidney cancer.

Done.

I called around and found a pancreatic surgeon at the same hospital and selected the head of the department. My initial impression was that he was a bit reserved, tall, handsome, with perfect posture and a formal bearing. I came to find out he was easy to talk to and really listened to me. I asked him at the first meeting if this hospital did many Whipples.

"We do about 230 here a year," he said.

"And I do about two-thirds of them myself," he continued.

Bingo!

The good news was that both surgeons agreed to take me on. As it turned out, they knew each other well, respected each other and had worked together many times.

Then I asked them separately if they would do the surgeries together on the same day. They both said yes, but with a caveat.

They both warned me that the Whipple would be first and if it went "seamlessly," Dr. Kidney would go in and take care of the kidney.

"If anything – *anything* – isn't perfect, we will wait to do the second surgery," Dr. Kidney said.

Everyone wants surgery to go well and now there was a second reason. I prayed that this double header could happen, saving me from going through one, waiting for recovery, then going in for the second.

It also meant going in for surgery not knowing if they would be doing both until I came out of anesthesia.

Both surgeons said their offices would coordinate to find a date. I was glad, but nervous. Now I knew that it could happen, I wanted to know when it would be.

I could only imagine how busy they were, and this was an all-day procedure for both, as Dr. Kidney would be standing by while Dr. Whipple cut out pieces of my digestive system and sewed together what was remaining in new arrangement.

Once the decision was made by both doctors to go ahead with a joint surgery, I was relieved, but the waiting was intolerable. The kidney cancer was there, it was in the pancreas as well as the kidney.

I didn't know how fast it was growing, but once I decided, I wanted to go ahead with it immediately.

At this point, it was mid-March. I had been in limbo since that dramatic Friday night in October when the kidney was screaming for attention.

Even though they said they would coordinate on a date, I couldn't wait for them. I decided to call both offices to see if I could arrange it. I would do it myself...the appointment, not the surgery.

On the March day I decided to make the calls, the pancreatic surgeon's office opened at 8:30 a.m., the kidney surgeon's not till 9. I called the pancreas office and talked to his nurse, who also scheduled his surgeries.

"He can only do it on Fridays and the only Friday he has open is April 22. We have to leave the whole day free."

I asked her to pencil me in, not knowing if I could even schedule a surgery. She seemed happy enough to do it. Protocol? I didn't know from protocol on these things.

That took all of two minutes. I watched the clock. When the big hand hit the 12 I called the kidney surgeon's office. He and his staff had always been wonderful to work with. I explained that both doctors had agreed to do the surgery. Could Dr. Kidney do the operation April 22 with Dr. Pancreas?

"Oh, we can make it work," the woman's voice on the phone said.

"Are you sure?"

How could she be sure? She certainly sounded sure, but had she taken the time to really check? I was incredulous. Did she know how long it would take? How Dr. Kidney could be waiting all day and then something would go wrong and it would be for nothing?

Maybe I should be worrying a little more about what I needed. They were adults and could decide.

"This is his wife," she said. "We were talking about you over the weekend. The 22nd will be fine."

I was ecstatic, more excited than anyone about to be cut open has the right to be. Then I thought of something. That would be a holiday weekend. Was that on his calendar? Maybe they were going away with the family.

I called her back.

"Do you know that day is Good Friday? Will that still be all right? Are you sure?"

She actually laughed. "Don't worry. We'll make it work."

Once the surgery date was settled, the planets were lining up for me and I began to sort out the details. But there was a gigantic roadblock.

I knew where I would be the morning of April 22, but what would happen to my mother?

Who was watching out for Nuzzie?

6

Nuzzie

During all these months wondering about my own treatment, I was also fretting about my increasingly frail 90-year-old mother.

Her given name was Katherine, but she, along with most of the Katherines, Katharines, Kathryns and Catherines of her generation, was known as Kay. When her first grandchild was born, she chose to be called Nuzzie. It had become what she called her own mother when she was just beginning to form words, calling impatiently from the crib: Mother, Muzzer, Nuzzer, Nuzzie!

The back story on my parents, Kay and Andy Tobin, was they retired to Florida in the 1980s after years in the Chicago area where my brother Chris and I had grown up. They had great fun playing golf, making friends, and were as happy and carefree as a couple of 65-year-old kids can be.

By now 20 years later, my dad had died and my mom needed my help with various medical situations, typical maladies of her stage in life. I was flying down to care for her and staying longer and longer each time.

Finally I insisted that she come up North with me. She was furious and told people I was kidnapping her. Eventually she got over it and was somewhat relieved, still not happy about losing her ability to take care of herself.

My mom stayed with me at my house for a few months, but it wasn't a permanent solution. I missed privacy, and she thought it was a pretty dull place. We agreed she needed more social life than I could provide. We looked for a place for her to live, with a peer group who appreciated Big Band music more than her daughter.

Nuzzie fell in love with an assisted living program we visited, signed on, and we had fun shopping for furnishings for what she called "the facility." She could still play an extremely competitive game of bridge at that point and she and her next-door neighbor Lila brought in players from the outside if residents didn't pass muster.

My mother soon turned into the unofficial ambassador there, slightly confused herself, but enthusiastically greeting newcomers and making them feel welcome.

Those years together in New England were good times for the two of us. We took long drives that reminded her of her native Vermont; my friends became her friends and she joined my book club. It was a gift to spend a lot of time with her at the end of her life and to broaden boundaries of the mother/daughter relationship.

I was the first person in my extended family to get cancer. Everyone else tended to have heart trouble and eventually succumb to it. Kidney cancer is relatively rare, and usually strikes men. I was beating the odds all around.

My mother sailed through a second hip replacement at 89 but her cardiac health continued to deteriorate and the worst of it coincided with my kidney/pancreas cancer diagnosis. She had had at least one TIA and was at high risk for major stroke. She had had congestive heart failure for years.

At one point, she ended up in the ER with a heart problem so severe that I was told to call the family and was asked whether she had a clergyman. At one point John, the minister from First Parish, my home church sat on the side of my mother's bed and held her hand, comforting both of us. OK, this is it, I thought.

When I was growing up, she told me I should "give her a powder" at 60, a phrase I didn't exactly understand but got the idea. She didn't really like old people, and now didn't want to think of herself as one of them.

My mother's brand-new cardiologist Dr. Heartwell was a gem. He told me that my mother probably wouldn't make it through that night but, on the other hand, if she did "she could live as long as six months." The words "six months" rang a little bell in my head.

Nuzzie did make it through that night, as she had many others before, and needed to move out of the hospital. She was off on another merry-go-round of trips to skilled nursing facilities followed by trips to the ER. She hadn't spent one night in her assisted living since December and it was now March.

She was clearly failing, with various medical problems, along with her heart. Her short-term memory on its way out, and she was sometimes delusional.

Who would go with her when I wasn't around to sit with her in the ER, talk to the doctors and try to figure out the next move? The game was constantly changing. Her beloved primary care physician couldn't treat her at the hospitals associated with her skilled nursing facilities.

I felt alone and nervous with the synchronicity of my cancer and my mother's severely failing health. I was feeling physically uncomfortable with the biliary stent that had been installed and was already having trouble with it that required replacement much more frequently than the predicted four times a year.

I was living alone, having divorced around the time of my initial kidney cancer surgery 12 years earlier.

My son was already plagued with anxiety before I was hit with the latest kidney news. Everything was complicated. My only sibling was in Chicago. My friends were great, but it was a lot to handle.

At this point my adult daughter had been in California for the past few years. Shortly after finishing college, she had moved to Berkeley. She had one foot out the door – her car was in our driveway, packed for the West Coast – when a major house fire hit one August night at 3 in the morning.

For both my kids, it was the only home they had ever known. My daughter was six weeks old when we moved into the house; my son was born two years later. We all had so many memories, of the holidays (my daughter said "Mom, you celebrate everything!"), birthday parties, just everyday life as a family. Her brother had learned to play the piano in that house and still loves to play.

My mother had the bad fortune of visiting from Florida the night of the fire. My son carried her down the stairs and outside, my daughter jumped into the hydrangea bushes from the second floor and ran to the neighbors to call for help. My son came back upstairs to find us and he and I got down by the firefighters' ladder. The four of us got out, though our lovely yellow Labrador retriever was lost.

It would be 18 months until the turn-of-the-century house was finally fully renovated.

Feelings of being a negligent daughter and an unreliable mother were mixed in with wondering how I was going to be able to take care of myself. Guilty, worried and scared all combined to leave me feeling frantic, which would be a good word to describe that time in general.

One immediate concern was how to get my mother in a safe situation. She did not want heroic measures, or anything to keep her alive, so why was she still going to the ER at all? I didn't exactly get that. I did know a requirement for hospice is that a physician needs to attest that the person in question has a life expectancy of six months or less.

There are few residential hospices in our area. I visited one of them, a gorgeous 18th-century place with fountains and gardens. I could imagine Martha Stewart photographing it for the cover of her new magazine, *Heaven-sent Hospice*: *It's a Good Thing.*

Would the doctor sign off on a hospice placement? Dr. Heartwell said he would. I told myself my mother would be well cared for, she would be safe, and she would be in a clean, beautiful place. I tried to shake off the feeling that I was dropping her off to die.

I talked to the director. The average length of stay was 15 to 20 days. They were full at the moment. "Openings come up," she said.

The director called me the very next day, and a bed had become available overnight. My mother's insurance would cover the entire cost. Unheard of.

But how could I break it to my mother that she was going to a hospice? As it turned out, I just never used the word, just moved her right in.

I went to see her as often as I could; my own energy was waning and my worries were escalating. I was impatient to rid myself of the tumors I was carrying around. My friends were wonderful at taking care of me, and they visited my mother in hospice. I breathed a big sigh of relief, silently promising her I would take over again as soon as I was out of the woods myself.

The hospice staff was great to her. The cooks only had eight patients to cook for, and several of the residents were not well enough to eat regular meals. They were happy to make Nuzzie whatever she wanted for dinner – many nights it was two strawberry sundaes with whipped cream and nuts.

With the move to hospice, Nuzzie was even more confused and easily agitated. I assumed telling her I would be going away could increase her growing disorientation. I was wrong. A week before my own hospitalization I mentioned I was going for minor surgery and I would come back soon. She didn't seem to be bothered, certainly not worried.

The good thing was that she liked everyone she met; that was her nature. And the staff was reassuring.

I had been desperate, and now an inner voice echoed theirs and told me Nuzzie was in good hands.

7

The whole abdominal extravaganza

About two weeks before the Whipple, I was instructed to go into the hospital for the four- to six-hour pre-op intake.

First of all, what could possibly take so long? And couldn't they just do the surgery while I was there, in that length of time? Please.

But it was quite the big deal, much like college registration with one stop after another and follow the yellow brick road, a line on the floor. I answered questions and was given tests all along the way.

It was a lot less taxing than the SAT, however, and it wasn't timed. Name and birthdate were confirmed at every juncture. I had been through this before, but I still didn't believe it could eat up almost an entire day. It did.

At the first stop, I was handed a tablet with questions about everything – current physical condition, health and surgical history, seemingly-random extremely personal questions, all leading up to the corker. "Are you worried about your sex life after surgery?

Now, what is the right answer? If yes, is that good because it indicates I think I'll live long enough for it to be a concern? If no, does that mean that I am so extraordinarily confident, so great in that department that nothing could possibly be a hindrance? Or is it that I think I probably won't survive the surgery anyway?

There was an EKG, there were blood tests, urine tests. Then it was on to the nurses. I love nurses. They are such practical people. This one was great. She kept me laughing as we went through item upon item.

"Oh, I see you're having the whole abdominal extravaganza," she said.

That made me proud. "Yes, I am."

That would be me.

"So you are going to have one surgery after another."

I explained to her there were two different surgeons.

"I didn't want to have pancreas surgery and then kidney surgery spread over a few months so I asked if I could have them the same day and they both said they would try."

I explained how if the Whipple went perfectly, the cutting and pasting of organs to the small intestine, yes. The kidney surgeon would then come in and take the tumor out of the kidney. If anything was a concern, the kidney portion of the extravaganza would be saved for after I recovered from the Whipple. If I woke up. Oops, don't go there.

Next item on the agenda: my beautiful nails. My beautiful totally fake French manicure that allowed me to unscrew screws without a screwdriver and never needed a touch up – until two weeks had passed and then they looked god-awful.

"No nail polish."

Well, I understand that in concept, because fingernails can give an idea what's going on inside. They aren't the windows to the soul (that would be the eyes), but if they are pink and turn blue, that isn't good. And if the nails are hiding under a coat of plastic, who knows what's happening? The indicator is gone. Did I want to have them removed? Absolutely not.

And I told her so. Yes, I have beautiful nails and, yes, I buy them every two weeks. I expected her to give me all the reasons I shouldn't have them. I was wrong.

"Just yes them to death and then forget about it. The day of the surgery no one will even notice."

Okay, then.

"Bring some crappy flats."

"What?"

"Yeah, you can't imagine what can happen to shoes in a hospital. Splattered on, leaked on, and bled on. Trust me on this one."

I mentally took a tour of my closet. I would have guessed it wouldn't be hard to sacrifice almost any pair to the cause. But what I came up with was this would be the perfect place to wear my Crocs.

The best part of the intake was getting my pancreatic surgeon's advice: "Gain five pounds [before the big day].You are going to lose a LOT of weight."

Talk about a silver lining! My primary care doctor almost fell off the chair laughing when I told her that one.

But I left the hospital and cheerfully followed the one order I thought was most important. I had an eating good time following my surgeon's advice and arrived back, Whipple ready, five pounds heavier.

And with 10 gorgeous acrylic nails polished with a French manicure.

8

The Whipple Brunch

With the intake behind me, there was one more thing
that had to happen, other than wait another two
weeks. What I knew for sure was that there was one
thing that would not get done. That would be filing
every scrap of paper in the house.

On the neatness scale, my house falls somewhere
between "drop in anytime, the house is fine," to "somebody call the Board of Health."

The first floor is somewhat presentable. But I confess
to a problem with paper; it's the quantity. And I have
to say there are perfectly neat rooms in my house. I
just can't think of one. Oh, yes, the guest room.

I found out that I am notorious for my tote bag filing
system. Of course, I have real file cabinets, draw-

ers and other containers that hold files. But do I use them? Do I even think to look there? I try, but instead I end up with bags of odd paper, most with labels so cryptic even I don't know what's inside.

Before I was to go in for the Whipple, I loaded up a few of the tote bags, stashed them, and decided it was good enough – worst case, my heirs could deal with the contents.

I started putting together a guest list.

When anything momentous happens, I give a party. It could be a birthday, the arrival of an out-of-town guest everyone should meet, or no reason at all. I have people over a lot and they seem to like to come. They stay a long time and that's fine with me, too. My house isn't large, but it is welcoming and comfortable and works as a clubhouse, a good place to celebrate. I took it as a compliment when my friend Chris came for a spa week with me. I don't even have a jetted tub.

I was going to be out of commission for a while, and I wanted to be able to see my friends and also do something nice for them. I wanted to drink some Prosecco, eat good food and have a little fun.

A brunch would be perfect because I could put everything on the table – egg soufflés, fruit, bagels and other breads, smoked salmon, cream cheese, all kinds of desserts – at the same time, and let the chips fall where they may. Kind of like deciding to have the Whipple in the first place.

So I sent out invitations to the Whipple Brunch.

The party was set for 10 days before the surgery. It was Eastertime. I had pots of flowers, a fire in the fireplace, the house was presentable. The tote bags were under my bed.

I needed a very special centerpiece, something that fit the occasion, in addition to primroses in the ginkgo leaf wrought iron basket. I put a few pots of pansies on a tray, but that certainly wasn't it. This was no time for pansies – I had to be strong like a pit bull to face what was coming. A snarling live dog on the table wouldn't work, however.

My friend Marlene had sent me a card labeled "Spare Parts for Old Farts" with tiny plastic organs glued to it. These little organs would expand to 600 times their size if placed in (enough) water. I pulled off the kidney. I saved the heart, brain and ear because, well, you just never know when someone will need a replacement organ.

The local party store had a large inflatable carrot, which is roughly the shape of a pancreas. I glued the little deflated kidney onto the carrot. With stick-on letters I spelled out "Welcome to the Whipple Brunch" on the carrot. It made the perfect centerpiece. It wasn't not exactly clear to everyone what it was, because believe it or not, some people don't think "pancreas" when they see a carrot. But I thought it was pretty funny. Still, there was a hint of anxiety in the air. Some people who saw the greeting seemed a little taken aback, initially.

I actually had carefully avoided referring to the get-together as the Whipple Brunch to my friend Mary.

She has been one of my best friends for decades. We have worked together at three newspapers and she is practically a member of the family. Now she edits a medical journal.

Mary was convinced anyone, not just me, would be absolutely crazy to go for the Whipple; she thought I would be making the biggest mistake of my life. She had been to a couple of my doctor's visits, and the information she had hadn't changed her opinion on the subject.

Maybe I was afraid to bring it up; I just pretended it was a get-together like any other. It looked like a mess of scrambled eggs with the usual suspects in attendance.

Mary came in, got a cup of coffee, and then took a look at the centerpiece. As soon as she saw it, she realized why we were gathered on that particular day. She took me aside wanted to know what was going on and sincerely thought she could still talk me out of going ahead with it. She was being protective.

There were a ton of friends and a boatload of food. There were short speeches, toasts. We had healthy food, hearty food, and decadent food. A fair amount of wine was consumed.

People said nice things to me, about me, that day. I felt loved but a little self-conscious. Had I set up my own wake?

I had already leaned on people to drive me downtown, to keep me company, and I knew I would have to accept help.

Some things I knew about; others I would come to realize that I needed, and some things were done without my knowledge.

The all-girl party went well into the evening. At one point, there was a small bunch of us left lounging in the living room, picking at what was left of the chocolate cake and drinking coffee. When anyone says, "Let me know if there is anything I can do," I knew enough to pounce on it. Next to good health insurance and competent doctors, friends who are willing to help are essential. I actually think they are the miracle workers.

At the end of the day, I knew my dog would have a primary caretaker and a couple of back-ups just in case, volunteers would visit my mother in her new hospice, my transportation was arranged, advocates to talk with the doctors were drafted or volunteered. One intrepid person said she would like to be the one to send out emails on my condition – no one else fought her for that privilege.

What I didn't realize then was that I would have needs beyond my wildest dreams. One friend took up a collection for a new laptop so I would not have to get upstairs to my desktop. It was embarrassing and touching at the same time. I accepted it.

My job was to survive to pay everybody back.

Cleopatra on her barge could not have felt more buoyed up than I did at the end of that April Sunday. There was so much love, so many good feelings, and so much gratitude on my part.

I could deal with dialysis or diabetes.

It had been six long months since the Friday night when the pain first hit, months filled with testing and diagnoses and second and third opinions. I had spent time worrying, praying, meditating. I had also spent a lot of time with people I loved, people I like to talk to and listen to; I read a lot of good books. I was able to put it out of my mind at least some of the time, probably because I was sick to death of thinking about it.

The following week I did odds and ends. I went to visit my mom, saw some people, had a little fun. It was as if I were moving, and I guess in a sense I was.

I left the pansies on the dining room table the morning I went to the hospital. There were two envelopes next to them, one with my mother's name on it, one with mine. Our affairs were in order.

The brunch had been exactly the right medicine. It was time to be knocked out.

9

Email Update: Whipple Day, April 22

Hello, Everyone:

Andrea asked me to keep everyone updated on her condition. She had a very serious surgery today to remove the tumors that were detected in October.

The last thing she said, as she sat with her fellow inmates in matching clothing, was that she wasn't afraid of the surgery, just afraid she would wake up and no one would notice.

She went into surgery about 9 a.m. and was in recovery around 5:30. Doctors told Eileen that Andrea did as well as could be expected, which is a huge relief, and the double operation, the Whipple procedure as well as the partial removal of her right kidney, was a success.

She is expected to be out of it through the night while she recovers from the initial shock of the surgery. I will be sending out another email tomorrow with more information as it becomes available. I certainly have been holding my breath all day and am beyond grateful and relieved that the first hurdle has been so successfully crossed.

She told me last night how much everyone's positive thoughts and prayers meant to her and how thankful she is to have so many people in her life pulling for her.

Alison

10

Absent-minded

In the early hours following the Whipple, I was floating. What happened to the worrier? For that matter, what happened to the worries?

Could it have been a meditation practice, the calm of a resilient spirit, friends taking such good care, or just giving in to the inevitable? No. It is a riddle. What begins with A and ends with A and...I forget.

Anesthesia was introduced in Boston at Massachusetts General Hospital in 1846. The ether dome, as it is called, is preserved to this day...with stadium seating. It is a true operating theater. Today's anesthesiologists have a lot to live up to, with this artifact on the top floor of the Bullfinch Building.

Before: The relief of going to sleep, with the knowledge that the next day will be the first step to recovery.

After: The bliss of floating, the only mental anxiety the inability to retrieve words, the memory loss. That's what friends are for.

After the Whipple, I was asked the name of the president of the United States. I came up with Barack but not Obama, or maybe Obama and not Barack. I've forgotten that, too. I think it took another day to be able to name the current year.

There is a rumor that I said I was the Great Pumpkin and my doctors came to find me in the pumpkin patch.

I don't remember if I was told if they had been able to remove part of my right kidney. I'd find out soon enough.

I felt no urgency to go home or even be at home. I was in a crib and was allowed to drift off to sleep whenever the urge struck me. I could push the morphine pump every seven minutes.

I woke up in pain and told the nurse I had had a bad night because I only remembered to hit the pump a couple of times. No wonder!

She told me the records showed 47 hits.

Oh, well, back to sleep.

11

Email Update: Whipple Plus Two

Hello, Everyone:

It is about 10:40 p.m. and I am sitting with Andrea while she snoozes. She had a great day today I am told. She got up and walked around twice and has been conversing very lucidly for most of the day.

Around 8 p.m. she started to spike a fever of 102 and became a little confused. The nurses gave her some Tylenol and sent some blood and urine samples to be tested. Her fever is continuing to come down and she is resting comfortably now. I feel much better now that I have seen her. Her color is great and despite the tubes and hospital surroundings she looks great!

Andrea's roommate shows Pomeranians and poodles in agility competitions so we are working on getting the room sanctioned as dog friendly so we can bring Cassie in for a visit. If that does not work (I am not holding my breath), the hospital allows good will ambassador therapy dogs to visit patients on Thursdays so both Andrea and her roommate will get their canine fix.

More information as it becomes available.

Hope you had a great Easter!

Alison

12

Nurses don't wear johnnies

The line between dreams and reality blurs when you are in the same bed day and night, awakened at odd hours. It's really a good strategy to assume you have to be ready for anything and be good-natured. Extra help will be there if you need it, fastest if the nursing staff hasn't identified you as the patient from hell.

One of the nights in the Big Hospital my friend Marlene slept in the recliner, also called a geri-chair, in my room. It must have been late. I don't know what time it was, but the lights were dimmed and it was quiet on the floor, aside from the usual beeping and shuffling of feet. No codes were going off, no fire alarms, no sprinkler systems activated.

I became aware someone had come into the room and was standing at my bed. The person didn't say anything to me, but that wasn't unusual. Suddenly I felt a hand under my pillow and soon there was a rummaging, accompanied by mumbling. She – and I had figured out it was a she, not a he – was feeling around more vigorously, as if she were looking for something.

After a few seconds of being shoved around, I asked her what she was doing. She didn't answer. She started pushing harder, moving me this way and that, and I wasn't getting it. She wasn't getting it, either. Her muttering picked up by a decibel or two. By this time it was more of a rant.

I could tell she was older, so I tried to be gentle with her.

"What exactly are you doing?" I asked.

"I'm looking for the pocketbook!"

Huh?

When she started pulling one of the blankets off me, I called Marlene, waking her up to see if she could assist.

Marlene looked over, bolted upright, and in one leap was beside my bed. Later Marlene told me her first thought was, "Nurses don't wear johnnies."

She came over and asked the woman what her name was.

"I'm Mrs. Evelyn Cabot Winthrop Lowell, I live on Beacon Hill and I want to know where my pocketbook is."

Marlene asked her where her room (at the hospital!) was.

"This is my bed and I want to know what happened to the pocketbook. Where is it? I want it now!"

Marlene buzzed for backup.

"This is Andrea's bed," Marlene told her. "Your pocketbook isn't here. Where is your room?"

Suddenly Mrs. Lowell turned on her.

"Now I suppose you're going to say *I* took it, aren't you? Now you're going to blame it all on me! That's what always happens, *doesn't it?*"

At this point Marlene was gently guiding her to the door. Gently wasn't cutting it, though, as she was determined to strip my bed – and possibly me – in her quest for the purse. Marlene and Mrs. Lowell were in a sort of dance, two steps toward the door and one step back toward my bed.

It seemed like forever, but two minutes later by the clock a nurse came to rescue Evelyn, and us, and take her back to the bed she came from.

I made a mental note not to keep anything under my pillow, now that I know it is the first place that nurses in johnnies look for their own stolen merchandise.

13

Book cart blockade

After one day on the operating table, another day trying to come up with the day of the week, I was deemed literally ready to roll.

After a morning lesson with the walker, I was released from my bed. I did have to have someone with me, anyone who was willing, and could go 50 feet in any one of two directions.

In a couple of days I had graduated to flying solo. It was me, the walker, the IV and the open road. The hallway beckoned. Whipple plus three days, I was up and down the linoleum when suddenly I could hardly put one foot in front of the other. I had the desire to go back to my room and lie down. Soon it was obviously more than a desire: It was get there or fall down where I was.

The door to my room was blocked by a woman with the book cart. Now, book carts are a wonderful amenity, especially at the Big Hospital, because unlike other medical venues you can take whatever appeals to you and you are not allowed to give it back.

This is in delightful contrast to the typical waiting room scenario, where if you are in the middle of an interesting story or want to get a recipe, you are forced to take the magazine to the bathroom and flush the toilet to cover the sound of ripping the pages out. And then there's the old bundle-it-under-your-coat routine.

No, these publications are yours. It must be great fun for the volunteer to spread the literature to the unhealthy masses and be benefactress of so much joy at no cost to herself.

A book cart is a wonderful thing, and so is a well-meaning volunteer driving it, but in this case the former was blocking my way and the latter was suffering a severe hearing loss.

I hobbled as fast as I could hobble, considering I was in real danger of passing out. I asked the volunteer to let me pass. Nothing. A little louder: "Please, I need to get into my room, I'm lightheaded."

Finally: "Hey, will you move it? Get out of the way, just GET OUT OF THE WAY!" She appeared startled, yet she seemed to have no interest in moving quickly.

Hospital volunteers aren't used to being shouted at, apparently. They aren't afraid of being fired.

But finally she inched the cart with just enough room for me to push myself and my paraphernalia through the door, past my roommate, to the bed where I could eventually fling myself .

I didn't pass out, but I was shaking violently. I don't remember ever being so cold, not even when the furnace went out in February.

Someone gave me a cup of tea. Wait a minute, where was I, Oxford? A cuppa could not have cured what ailed me. I was shaking so violently that when I took the cup the tea flew all over the bedcovers.

I was given a heated blanket, and another, and another until there were five. They made absolutely no difference.

All of a sudden the room was filled with people yelling and pushing each other out of the way. Someone literally ran into the room with a portable X-ray machine. I thought I must be dying. Either that or on the set of a hospital TV show.

I was afraid to close my eyes because I thought I might never open them again. Eileen, who had been sitting in the geri-chair, came over and sat next to me and held my hand; we were both crying. I asked her if she knew the name of my lawyer (so I could put her in my will). She didn't. I told Eileen the name and asked her to memorize it because I was afraid for her to let go of my hand to get a pen.

I don't know what they gave me, but at some point the shaking stopped. The desire to close my eyes was irresistible. Did I still think I would die? Oh, yes, but now I didn't care.

A nurse was screaming in my face, "Look me in the eye!"

I just wanted her to go away.

"Make eye contact!"

I tried, but couldn't. I had never been so tired in my whole life. The next thing was that she would start slapping me. Slap away, I thought. Now I know she was trying to keep me from losing consciousness.

I don't know what happened next. I did go to sleep. And I woke up.

But at the end of the day, what was that, what just happened? Pneumonia was the diagnosis. Really? I thought pneumonia was a gradual process starting with a cold, weeks of coughing, maybe a month of wondering whether to make an appointment with the primary care doctor, finally going in. I didn't ask questions.

They were finally letting me slumber in my hospital bed. Have I ever loved a bed more?

It was heaven. But in a good way.

14

Email Update: Pneumonia

Hello, Everyone:

I did not write yesterday because I did not get to see Andrea until 10 p.m. and at that point she was so awake and energetic we had what can best be described as a slumber party in her hospital room until I fell asleep in a recliner.

The doctors finally figured out why she had a cycling fever. They determined that she has pneumonia so they put her on an IV antibiotic. They are not overly concerned about the pneumonia because it is easily treatable. They are very relieved she does not have another kind of infection. They have not yet determined where she will be going to rehab.

I know I keep saying how well she is doing, but just this morning her doctor said that she should be the poster girl for the Whipple because she has exceeded all their expectations. It is just so exciting! Her diet is not very exciting yet, but she has started to eat solid foods, albeit bland foods.

More information as it becomes available,

Alison

15

When love comes knocking

My time in the hospital was a hurry-up-and-wait situation. There were blood draws, IVs, medications, vitals checked, changes to those medications, nurses coming in to check pain levels, lots of questions, and little interrupted sleep.

Because the Big Hospital is a teaching hospital, the day started while it was dark outside. Lights went on, several pairs of feet in clogs clumped in, I was peppered with questions. Before I knew it, they were out of there and the visitors slowed to a trickle.

Once I got out of bed after the surgery there was a lot of hall roaming, first with help, then alone, and lot of time and opportunities to make observations.

For example, there is the closed door in the corridor labeled Lovenox Closet. What evil or ecstasy resides in the Lovenox Closet? When this mysterious brand of love knocks, it is probably better not to answer.

Another oddity was the open-top bins mounted high on the walls, full to overflowing with syringes. Why would they be there for the taking? For easy access if a doctor was flying down the hall and needed to inject someone on the double? There were two different kinds, maybe one for bee stings and the other for a quick recreational fix? All were wrapped in cellophane, so I wasn't worried about the sterility factor.

In my trips between hospitals I spent a lot of time in emergency rooms, now called emergency departments. There is nothing to do but wait. Despite the name, there is nothing fast-paced about them, unless you are gushing blood. And even then! Anyway, there are always a lot of carts transporting supplies, patients. Everything is on wheels. And what is a SANE cart?

So many questions, so at one point I cornered a nurse who would surely be in the know.

"What is the reason for the syringes everywhere? Isn't it dangerous to leave them out like that?

"You're right," he said. "And maybe we should get the bowls of Percocet off the counter."

Oh. Okay.

"Sharps" are what they sound like, and they are not in the syringes, it turned out. And Percocet is locked up.

The sexy Lovenox turns out to be medication to prevent deep-vein thrombosis.

And the SANE cart is for victims of sexual assault.

No more questions.

16

Tiaras, 4-oz. ginger ale, and doctor-assisted cupcakes

In the olden days, children could not visit their parents in the hospital, patients with serious medical conditions were shielded from the awful truth, and if you wanted to watch TV in your room you had to pay for it.

Now TV is free, and we don't need to thank Obamacare for that improvement in the quality of patient care. It's probably a good thing, because it seems that you get what you are paying for. Let's face it, in every way that matters, you would have more entertainment choices flying Jet Blue than recuperating from surgery.

Who doesn't love Lucy? And who hasn't seen every episode? At the Big Hospital they must subscribe to about 10 of the classic episodes. These are then burned into your brain, creating a sort of twilight sleep about your stay there.

There's the one where Lucy and Ethel decide to produce their own salad dressing and promote it on TV. In those pre-infomercial days, it's like looking at cave paintings. Then there's the time the Mertzes buy the Ricardos' old washing machine and it proves to be no bargain.

One of my favorites is the one in which Lucy and Ricky plan a road trip to California and take Ethel and Fred along, or attempt to until the car they've purchased for the vacation breaks down curbside in front of their apartment building.

Lucy and Ricky's New York apartment became more familiar to me than my own first house. You could sense Lucy's claustrophobia in that apartment and her constant desire for the glamorous life she had hoped to become accustomed to. She found adventure with her own overactive imagination, much to the frustration of her Cuban bandleader husband Ricky, setting off his volcanic temper. He shouted, she cried. Time to change the channel.

There were also several sports stations, along with "Say Yes to the Dress." This was a favorite in the room I shared, featuring brides selecting wedding gowns with the "help" of assorted in-laws and sisters who brought along a generous helping of sibling rivalry bordering on smoldering hostility. Occasionally a fiancé would show up; clearly these men had never seen the show. The bridegrooms-to-be evoked the most tears, never tears of joy, from the bride.

When the TV popped on, it was always the in-house
program about the hospital's recent impressive anniversary and its accompanying commemorative book.
With footage of old photographs of patients in iron
beds there were interviews of current volunteers and
staff. The part I liked best was the author of the book
talking about his writing process. With his self-depre-
cating manner, boyish good looks and argyle socks, he
hinted at being drawn and quartered by the compet-
ing demands of every living soul in the hospital. He
compared it to "being on 10 leashes."

Then there was Jerry Springer. I hadn't seen his
show before and haven't looked for it since. It seemed
to always deal with questions of paternity and no-
holds-barred fights. The program began with a tearful
explanation of the problem by the seemingly injured
party, the injustice experienced and then the he-said,
she-said. Gloves inevitably came off, despite security
guards circling the guests. Finally, full wigs were
ripped off heads in the crescendo.

We had to wonder what the participants got out of
this. And, because my friend Eileen and I had a lot of
time on our hands and a little technology, we took our
questions to the Internet on her smartphone. According to what we could find out, the payoff was a train
trip to the studio and one night in a hotel. And maybe
justice was served.

But TV watching at the Big Hospital wasn't just an
endless reel of Lucy and Ricky and in-house puffery.

I had the incredible good fortune to be there for the
week preceding The Wedding of the Century, the

marriage of the beautiful commoner with the glossy chocolate mane to her fair-haired prince, heir to the crown of the United Kingdom.

Ask me anything about the wedding of Kate and Wills. I saw it all. The theme music was the soundtrack to my recuperation.

Eileen spent most of the days with me the week leading up to the event and she saw it all, too. She had her recliner, the best one on the floor, which she turned over to whoever was replacing her as my babysitter when she went home. That much-coveted chair was sometimes sneaked into my room when guests of other patients were gone for the night, or even down in the cafeteria. It had to be there for the wedding. Who says the sun never sets on the British Empire? That recliner was more closely watched by my posse of friends than the infants in the NICU.

I, of course, was guaranteed a front row seat because as a patient I had a TV and a remote. As did my roommate. We had two TVs in our room, but we shared a brain. She was a dog person, I was a dog person. We talked about our dogs endlessly. We voted on wedding dresses, we complained about Ricky's insensitivity to his admittedly crazy red-haired wife. (The reruns were all in black and white, but we knew Lucy's hair was red the same way everyone knew Lassie's was golden.)

The Sunday before The Wedding of the Century was Easter that year. There was candy everywhere. One of the nurses told me they had had an egg hunt in the hall. We knew we were in the right place. There was a rumor that all three of us Whipple patients were on that floor, so how could it not be Fun Central? And what was Easter compared to the wedding?

On Thursday of Wedding Week I decided I needed to get my hair done. I couldn't very well get a chi-chi British fascinator to wear on my head, but I could have a good hair day. One of the nurses told me they used to have special shampoo caps but she hadn't seen them for years. Someone located it stuck in the back of a closet in a dusty cardboard box. Who knew you could clean your hair without getting near a sink, or even water? The directions said to pop it into the microwave; that was encouraging. If it needed a microwave it couldn't be much older than 1980.

"Here you go," the nurse said, handing me the cap after she nuked it. I put it on and could feel a little moisture.

"Now massage it."

After the recommended number of minutes I took it off. My hair was soaking wet and squeaky clean. The inside of the cap was filled with god-knows-what gray stuff.

All I needed was a blow dry. I would come to learn the best nurses are former hairdressers and on that day one of them took over my hair. I was stylin.'

Someone needed to buy favors, though. Eileen and I made a list and she went shopping. I wasn't this excited when I got married myself. Eileen got me a crown any 3-year-old would die for. It was pink. It had feathers. There were "diamonds."

The wedding coverage was starting in earnest at 4
a.m. Friday morning and I was ready, crown on my
head. Four a.m. is a time to wake up in a hospital
anyway, so I was all set. Eileen said she'd pass on the
hype – as if!

"You can wake me up at 5," she said.

I promised I would.

A true friend, Eileen had bought a raft of tiaras. They
were all a little downsized from mine, pale versions of
my flamingo pink number. The nurses all wore them,
even the men. My roommate and her sister had them
proudly on their heads.

In the spirit of the celebration we were all offered
half-pints of ginger ale, a breach of dietary restric-
tions. One of the surgery fellows made glittery cup-
cakes and passed them around.

We watched all the build-up, the crowds, the endless
commentary, the speculation about the dress, the
arrival of Kate wearing the lace gown. Lip readers
were called in to see what Harry said to his brother
when the bride walked toward them ("she's here") and,
later, Kate's comment when she looked down at the
crowd surrounding Buckingham Palace ("oh, wow").

It was glorious. I watched every minute and called my
friend Marion in Ireland so we could compare notes
as it happened. Her sisters and nieces were all there,
gathered around her TV in County Wexford.

"Be who God meant you to be and you will set the
world on *faaar*," the Bishop of London solemnly told
the royal couple, quoting St. Catherine of Siena.

Of course I knew the wedding day was the feast day of St. Catherine. As I said, ask me anything. I credit the morphine for my endless fascination in seeing the same footage over and over and over again. I actually couldn't get enough of it.

It didn't matter that I couldn't eat the cupcake, by the way, or drink the ginger ale. I had my crown and was filled with the joy of the occasion.

It just couldn't get any more thrilling.

Or could it?

The next day would prove to be unforgettable, the literal high point of any of my hospital stays.

17

Email Update:
The First Week

Hello, Everyone:

I have spent the day with Andrea. She looks great, the doctors continue to be thrilled with the surgery and her recovery progress, and her room is rapidly filling up with the most beautiful flowers…as I typed that sentence an adorable delivery man brought in the sweetest addition to her indoor garden J. Seriously, the flowers are so gorgeous and smell of spring. I always think of Andrea surrounded by her garden so I can't think of a better way to make her feel comfortable.

She is officially off dialysis and if everything continues to improve she will not need it at all. One of her biggest concerns was the prospect of dialysis three days a week and it is a wonderful relief that this is no longer a concern.

She spent a couple of hours sitting up today and watched the best that daytime television has to offer: Jerry Springer, "Strippers Confess," Tyra Banks on "Child Actors" and Cake Boss.

She also got up and walked four times today and she met with the physical therapist.

It is very likely she will be going to a rehab facility sometime in the next week, although no decisions have been made yet.

All in all, things are looking very positive. She is a tough cookie.

More information as it becomes available.

Alison

18

Oxycodone and me

When I am in pain, Oxycodone is not my friend. Write that on my chart.

Percocet, on the other hand, is my bosom buddy. I wish I could be the person I am on Percocet. I don't feel high. I'm just the greatest person I ever met. I'm not the only one who reacts this way.

An extremely well-regarded radio commentator returned to the air following a serious accident on the water. I don't remember what happened – maybe a shark got to her, maybe it was a boat propeller – and she probably doesn't recall either. Anyway, her first day back on the air she thanked her loyal listeners... and Percocet. I couldn't believe it. Now, really, what did her loyal listeners do for her that Percocet hadn't done in spades?

There is one problem with Percocet in my experience. I don't want to talk about it, except that a fraction of one pill causes the lower half of my body to turn to lead. I'm not the only one who has this reaction, either.

I'm not anti-medication, pro-pain. Not at all. I refused Percocet and was given Oxycodone. I had never tried it, why not? That was the street drug I thought would make me feel lighthearted and free. Wrong. It made me feel crazy. And not in a good way.

The day I was to move over to Oxycodone from morphine my brother stopped in from Chicago for a visit. Chris loves what he does, particularly his public service projects. He describes how he finds actors, chooses the music, sometimes *writes* the music, directs, and produces.

We talked that day of how I might use my work experience and go off in a new direction.

After he left, it was time for my first dose of Oxycodone. A little time passed, I don't know how much, but pretty soon I had a blast of insight. I decided I would make a movie, not a little TV movie, but really think big. I could get a bunch of money from the equity in my house – *hell, all the money.*

I would buy the rights to some obscure, heretofore unnoticed, brilliant book and make it into a major motion picture. It would clear at least 20, 40, 60 million bucks. more than I could make in several lifetimes, that was for sure.

All I had to do was buy the rights, get some actors together, and find someone to write the screenplay. I had written a screenplay once, I could do this one and make even more money. It would be so easy. Piece of cake.

I looked for the phone number of my mortgage holder, but it wasn't in the tray table or the pocket of my johnnie, if there even was a pocket. If only I had my checkbook with me. I was sure there was a list of properties and I just had to choose one. Who had the list?

Why hadn't I thought of this before? I blissfully drifted off to sleep with visions of picking up my award on Oscar night, music from the score playing along with the applause of the ecstatic audience.

The next day, still on the Oxy, I got a text message telling me I needed to edit a 60-page document. I was worried that I couldn't get it finished. I was in a panic, in fact. I had to be done by midnight and the lack of computer was slowing me down. I told the nurse about it.

"Who sent the document to you," she asked.

Who sent it to me? How stupid was she? How would I know who sent it to me?

"Okay, then."

She didn't press the issue.

"Where do you need to send it? Maybe I can help you."

I didn't know that either. What did that have to do with anything? Why was it important? I just knew if she didn't stop with the small talk I would never get it done.

My eyes were closing. It would have to wait, that is just all there was to it. Maybe I would be cut a little slack because I was in the hospital. And I did know that much; I was in the hospital and deadlines were closing in on me. Somehow, even with all the deadline pressure, I managed to fall asleep.

The third and last time I took Oxycodone I suddenly realized the entire floor of the hospital was empty. Eerily empty. Deadly silent. No anybody.

Wait a minute. Mary was there, whispering in my ear, asking me what medication I was on and what the dosages were. Why was she here, and why was she so unconcerned about the fact that some sort of body-snatchers had taken every living person, with the exception of the two of us?

I just wanted Mary to stop. I tried to call security. The phone was gone. No cops. Not a creature was stirring.

Maybe it was a good reason, a celebration, or some special occasion. Maybe it was someone's birthday, or the unit had hit some kind of quota that I really didn't want to know hospitals had. Could it be a lockdown, a terrorist attack?

Then I found out what happened: Everyone had gone to the Outback Steakhouse. Why was Mary here, then?

Aha! *Mary didn't eat red meat.* It was all beginning to make a little sense.

That was the last time I had Oxycodone. The next day I had the nurse (who said she had not been to the Outback) put it down on my chart as an allergy.

I realized I was better at handling the lows in my life than the highs.

19

Ambulance drivers

Eventually I was discharged from the Big Hospital
to go to a transitional care unit, a rehab, at a Little
Hospital close to home. I had to pack up a surprising
amount of stuff. As I was about to leave, Dr. Whipple/
Pancreas stopped by to see me.

"Look at these flowers! There are so many," he said

At that time there were enough flowers for a funeral,
well maybe a funeral for a non-celebrity who had lived
a long life.

"Oh, yes, this is the Little Shop of Horrors," I said,
referring to the iconic film about the carnivorous
plants in a florist's shop.

"I don't know why you would say that," he said, just as
I remembered he hadn't grown up in this country.

"Oh, that was a joke. It was a movie."

"Well, *I* think they're lovely," he said.

I agreed with him. Some things are best lost in translation.

Along with the flowers, there were a few other items, some bulkier than others. I had special blankets, my memory foam mattress, notebooks, books, sweaters, magazines, all the comforts of my hospital home.

Two transport guys arrived, already playing good cop, bad cop.

Eileen, who had had her car packed, asked good cop Sean if we could put the flowers in the ambulance, and he said it would be fine as long as they fit.

His partner, John, who had been just outside my room, came in to pick up the primary cargo that weighed, well, let's just say somewhere between 100 and 200 pounds.

"Those ain't comin' with us," he said, scowling at a vase of particularly lush and extremely odiferous stargazer lilies. I wanted to say the lilies had medicinal qualities as smelling salts but decided he had no sense of humor. And if he was the driver I didn't want to give him any cause for road rage.

Eileen retrieved what John refused and followed the ambulance the 20 or so miles to the Little Hospital. It was an impressive array, even after leaving a couple of arrangements for the nurses.

We went down in the elevator to the ambulance entrance. The sky was sparkling clear. We drove along the Charles River and crossed over. There were sailboats. I had a delicious feeling of freedom, even strapped in the ambulance, even with a partially obstructed view. I was going to the country.

John, the cranky one, did turn out to be the driver, so I didn't have contact with him, but the other one sat in the back with me. Sean was a twenty-something paramedic who was in a fast-track program to get a nursing degree in one year.

When I asked him what he wanted to do with the degree, he immediately said he wanted to be a traveling nurse.

"I can stay one place for three months, and then move for three months, or work in a place full-time. Dublin is one place that pays well, the second highest salary after Japan. And I'd like it there, with the pubs and all," he said.

We got going on the subject of travel.

It turns out that Sean had spent all his spare time and money going places. He had wanderlust in his heart, a boy after my own heart. We had a great conversation about travel highlights, everywhere from Istanbul to Santiago and lots of places I knew nothing about.

He filled me in, giving me even more reasons to get over this pesky recuperation and expand my world. I had been doing travel writing newspapers for years and wasn't ready to abandon it forever.

Our vehicle arrived at the Little Hospital too soon. Driver John seemed in much better humor and together they unloaded me, tucked in some of the plants and wheeled me to my room.

Could I just get Sean on the payroll, have him signed on as an aide where I was headed? I wanted to see pictures from his trips. But, no, once I was safely in my room, John and Sean, Frick and Frack, got back on the road to return to Boston.

I didn't know then that I would soon have the good fortune to meet Dave, a nurse for all reasons.

20

Dave, a nurse for all reasons

Whee! I arrived at my room in the Little Hospital rehab unit to find it was private. I would be all alone.

There had been a standoff with social services at the Big Hospital. When I was ready to be discharged, I needed intermediate care in some kind of rehab. I was given a list to choose from, but I really wanted to go to the transitional care unit at the community hospital that I knew well.

No nursing home for me, not if I could help it. I wanted to be in the 20-bed country club of transitional care units, the one with hydrangeas painted on the corridor walls and the three-star restaurant menu.

(Full disclosure: I had once worked at the Little Hospital as an intern in the in-patient psych unit after getting a mid-life master's degree in social work.)

Andrea Cleghorn

My room was large and light, and the view five stories below looked over a marsh and meandering river. It was late afternoon on a lush May day; it doesn't get much greener in New England.

It was peacefully quiet here, too. The city vibe of a big, busy hospital could get annoying if you were not totally doped up. The beep-beep-beep here was softer, the bells were more melodic. I desperately wanted to take a nap.

One tough thing about big-city teaching hospitals, of which Big Hospital is one of the largest at 1,000 beds, is the plethora of personnel. The team of bright-eyed, eager men and women in white coats arrives at 6 in the morning. They are bright, professional and efficient. As individuals, I became very fond of many of them. As a group, at that hour? Hated them all!

At any rate, I was in the leafy suburbs now.

Ambulance guys Sean and John had no sooner dropped me off than I had a visit from my nurse, Maybelle, who was just going off shift. She was pleasant. She took my vitals, checked my tubing, asked me a few questions, including if she could get me anything. I didn't think so. I certainly didn't need or want her to scour the premises for a roommate.

I desperately wanted a nap, and I was certain I wasn't the only one. It took two trips for Eileen to bring my belongings from her car, parked five floors down and at the other end of the hospital. It must have been beginning to remind her of our trek up Skellig Michael all those months earlier. She looked exhausted. In addition, she had been on the night

100

shift rotation the last few nights, sometimes getting
a bed in the hospital but often sleeping in a geri-chair/
recliner.

Eileen put away what she could, leaving a pile of
plants in a corner of the room.

"Would you mind if I go home?" she asked me. "Will
you be all right?"

I told her to please go, reminding myself that I could
never, ever repay her for all she was doing.

She lived 20 minutes of easy driving from this new
location, versus the hour-plus with traffic she had
been coping with in traveling to the Big Hospital. We
were both relieved to get me closer. I had also reached
a level of recovery where nobody felt they had to stay
with me overnight.

A new nurse came along with the shift change. This
one was adorable, young, energetic, cute and male. I
never knew how tall anyone was, since I was always
in a prone position, not that it mattered. Dave was to
become my new best friend. He admired the plants
and asked me about them. How many people want to
read the cards, ask who sent them, praise and nitpick?

The non-arrangement of planters in the corner
offended Dave's sensibilities. He looked around, went
out and came back lugging a table to put them on.
That still wasn't right. Where was the tablecloth?
What he accomplished folding a twin-size sheet was
impressive. I was half-expecting him to pull out a
needle and thread and stitch an ornamental border, or
at least draw a design with a sharpie pen. But he got

it all set, placing the table at an angle and fussing to get the plants just right.

We both admired his work. The pinks set off the dark foliage, and the trailing plant was spilling over just as God intended. Now: Did I need anything else, of a medical nature maybe?

While Dave was doing that, I had put a few things on my tray side table, including my phone, which I noticed was almost out of juice. I looked around for the charger. Dave looked. It was nowhere; it must have been left behind.

Have to say here that there are very few things you need to bring to a hospital. *Want* is one thing, but not *need*. If you need something, they have it. I personally think makeup is a necessity but not everyone agrees. In general, if they can't supply it, you don't need it.

There are, of course, a couple of exceptions beyond lip gloss and blush, one being dental floss. True. The other is a phone charger. I can call my own phone from a different phone and find it (assuming it's charged), but chargers do not have ringers. And generally medical institutions have signs everywhere saying cell phone use is prohibited. But does anyone view that policy as anything more than a suggestion?

A cell phone is a necessity. So is a charger.

I reluctantly called Eileen at home to ask her if she remembered seeing the charger, but her husband, Dick, answered the phone, saying she was already tucked in bed. He asked me if I needed anything. I told him what happened.

"Oh, I'll get you another charger. I can stop at Radio Shack and be right over."

"You're not doing anything?" I asked.

"No, which one do you need?"

Well, phones are like little snowflakes, it seems, each one special in its own way. I described the phone. Just then Dave showed up.

"Oh, let me take the phone apart and I'll look at the battery. It will have the model number and from there I can look on the Internet to see what charger it needs," he said.

He came back in a few minutes later, triumphantly waving a slip of paper with the information.

"I asked around to see if anyone had your phone with a charger you could borrow, but everyone has smart phones [except you]."

I called Dick back, feeling guilty, but knowing that I would need to have to have a charger, probably that night. I needed to get in touch with my daughter who was arriving from California the next day with her boyfriend. Until that morning, I wasn't sure where I would be.

He said he'd pick up a new one and bring it over.

All of a sudden, Dick appeared in my room. He had left his house, traveled three miles to Radio Shack, found the charger and paid for it, driven seven miles to the Little Hospital parking structure, found a spot for the car, gone into hospital, taken the elevator to my floor and walked in. It was 27 minutes since I had hung up with him.

Dick met Dave, the flip phone got plugged in, and Dick was on his way. I was on my way, too, safe, warm and connected to the world. And determined to upgrade my flip phone to something more intelligent.

I called my daughter, then fell asleep, pain meds in my system, the bed alarm turned on that night so I wouldn't wander off.

There was no one to call or anywhere to go except Slumberland.

21

Chihuahua on the floor: Bandit in a blanket

There are certain luxuries that a hospital can never provide. One, apparently, is a mattress covered in something softer than crinkly plastic. Another is a family member who shares no resemblance to you, even the number of legs.

What I missed more than anything from home was my comfy dog, my shaggy, 60-pound bundle who slept next to me every night at home.

The Little Hospital rehab was nice. It didn't have the edge of the Big Hospital in some ways, but who needs "edge" when recuperating? It offered free Reiki, the laying on of hands to promote healing, every day a patient wants it. But no therapy dogs.

It was funny because what I initially thought of as an advantage of the Big Hospital was Thursday,

Therapy Dog Day. These pooches were popular with patients, and I kept reminding the nurse not to skip my room. My first week after the Whipple, Thursday finally arrived.

An overzealous beagle named Fritz repeatedly tried to leap up and reach me. He looked as if he might make it.

His owner said, "Do you want me to put him in bed with you?"

"Err, no thanks," I said, instinctively covering my belly with both hands. I was horrified at the thought of this hound throwing himself on top of the massive belt of staples holding together my brand-new incision.

I never saw the next canine who was on duty that day, one with a deep, gravelly voice. I assumed he or she was on my floor working the other side of the corridor. I pictured that dog as an English mastiff.

Next up in my room was a sweet retriever who looked like she wouldn't hurt a flea. I've known this breed; they are lovely. They will also do anything for food. I've seen guide dogs sweep a movie theater floor clean of popcorn, gummy bears, Milk Duds, just in passing.

Miss Sweetiepie was ambling around, sniffing, giving my hand a lick. Her owner was dressed in a jaunty outfit and keeping up a southern-accented line of chat.

"Would you like to give Miss Sweetiepie a little treat?" she asked.

Of course I would.

I had two visitors at the time; we were all loving this gorgeous dog with her Hershey's kiss eyes. What came next was an accident, I truly believe that.

The dog was salivating as her owner slowly pulled a tiny Milk Bone out of her purse and handed it to me.

I gave it to the dog, not on the flat palm of my hand as you would a horse, but I held one end and the bitch immediately opened her enormous mouth.

Chomp! Next came a deafening yelp. From me. Three of us leaped from our seats. I jumped the highest and hardly dared look at my forefinger to see if it was intact. Her teeth had scraped me, but nothing was missing. The Milk Bone had disappeared down Sweet-iepie's throat. Her owner was unfazed. She just kept right on talking.

So my therapy dog experience at the Big Hospital had not been stellar.

But now I was at the Little Hospital rehab, still craving a visitor of the canine persuasion. This new place didn't allow therapy dogs of any kind. I really needed one.

My friend Alison, a dog walker by trade, tried to tell me about her new long-haired Chihuahua but couldn't really adequately describe his awesomeness. I'd heard about this client's gorgeous dark eyes, long hair and winning personality. His ears stuck out, more Dumbo than Obama. He and I had to hook up and it couldn't wait till I got home from the hospital.

We decided Alison would bring in Bandit. Since I had a private room, we would just take our chances. Visit-

ing hours for humans were generous; visiting hours
for dogs were nonexistent.

It was a quiet night. Alison walked right into my room
which was well-positioned, as she didn't need to pass
by the nurses' station to get there.

This cute young thing was everything she described
and more. I loved Bandit's coat more than anything.
We had to be discreet. Bandit was not welcome in this
hospital. He was the wrong species. He could have
had fleas. He didn't.

Now, there are a lot of hard edges in a hospital.
Everything is supposedly sterile, although it's easier
to catch some kind of bug there than perhaps anywhere else on the planet.

She had him under her own coat. She placed the little
Chihuahua in my bed. Soon we heard footsteps coming toward the room.

I handed Bandit and my prayer blanket to Alison
and she hurried over to a chair facing the window.
A golden paw stuck out of one side of the hand-knit
blanket, a silken ear out the other just as the offi-
cious nurse Maybelle came into the room. Alison sat
with her back to us over by the window in a position
designed to approximate nursing an infant.

The nurse was especially attentive that night. In and
out. Bandit wasn't totally buying into the nursing-
infant disguise and wanted to be put down. At one
point Alison rushed into the bathroom with him,
repeatedly flushing the toilet to disguise his various
squeaks and the pitter patter of tiny feet.

Alison closed the door to my room. That got me even more attention. It was opened in a flash, just enough time for Alison to go back to the window

"It's against hospital regulations to keep the door closed," Maybelle informed me. Alison, again in her breast-feeding mode, kept her back to the window, almost as if she were extremely modest or there was something fascinating out there in the dark.

I don't know how much Maybelle really knew. I think she was suspicious that we were having sex or taking recreational drugs. Whatever was afoot, she was on it. From my perspective, it was all good clean fun. That, and the desire to have one of the most comforting of the comforts of home.

This 4-pound dog was creating a high degree of stress in the room, however.

Eventually Alison packed him up under her coat and took him home.

Late that night the medical director came by and we were making small talk. I hinted at what happened. I thought she might think it was funny, though apparently not. She said she didn't want to know about it, or she would have to file a report. It would probably go on someone's Permanent Record – hers, mine, Alison's or Bandit's.

Poor little Bandit hadn't done anything wrong. Bundled in a blanket, he was a gentler relative of the enormous Miss Sweetiepie back at the Big Hospital who had accidentally bitten me. And superior in every way to the sausage dog Fritz who was determined to sit on my staples.

What a good boy Bandit was! Still, he wasn't ever invited back; the other three are probably still making the rounds downtown.

22

Email Update:
Back and Forth

Hello, Everyone:

Sorry for the interruption in updates. Andrea was doing really well and had been transferred to Little Hospital for rehab. As of Friday night she was upbeat, alert, eating, and enjoying her new private room with a view of the river and a beautiful table overflowing with cards and flowers.

At some point on Sunday she developed an infection and was sent back to the Big Hospital so her doctors could determine the best course to take. The situation is under control and I know we are all praying that this is only a minor and brief setback for her recovery. Doctors have put in a drain for fluids and will be inserting another stent later today. At this time she has requested no visitors. I should have a better handle on the situation later this evening and I will keep you all up to date on her progress.

Thank you all for your concern and support.

Alison

23

Mock: In the same vein

Open letter to Needle Inserters from a Tough Stick:

Because I have gained a reputation, I need to remind you that I may have bad veins but that does not mean that I am necessarily a bad person. And before the Whipple era started, I was pretty much an average stick, if you will.

I want to apologize to one and all for wrecking your day. It is honestly unintentional. Don't even go to that place where it hurts you more than it does me. And I would like to say, please don't fool around trying to impress me with your skill.

A disclaimer: most of you are nice, well-meaning folks. But if you aren't good at this, don't act as if this is the first time you've missed the mark. I'm going to find out the truth soon enough, and if you are trying to place the blame on me, well, it won't stick. I'll ask for your supervisor, or even higher. The Surgeon General would certainly be interested.

One of the effects of my intense siege in the hospital has meant that the old veins are not what they used to be. At times my arms just ached; raising them for a chest X-ray was torture. So one bright nurse had the idea to pull out a sharpie and draw circles with diagonal lines running through to warn "don't even think of sticking anything sharp here!" For some technicians, even that is not enough.

The Booby Prize goes to Perry, the black-haired, harried nurse. She came storming into my room one afternoon complaining about what a horrible day she'd had. Apparently she was determined that her patients all would have one, too.

She wasn't just glowing a bit with perspiration, the sweat was pouring out of this woman. She was mad as a wet hen, a soaking wet hen.

Perry ripped off her gloves and started slapping my arms. She seemed to have had a lot of practice in that department.

Somehow I knew she would be an alumna of the bare-arm tourniquet-tying school. Ouch and double ouch.

Perry couldn't find a vein, so she hustled off, mumbling something. I assumed she was calling for backup, but I really don't know what was going on. She left the needle in my arm, attached to nothing, while I frantically called and rang the bell for her to take it out. Forty-five minutes, or seemed like it. My forearm was expanding. When she finally returned I asked her to never, ever come back.

She did return, though, a couple of days later, peeking around the door. I reminded her I didn't want to see her ever again.

"Oh, I thought you wouldn't recognize me without your glasses," she said, as she very quietly left the room.

I must give credit to some of the good ones, the true greats, candidates for the IV Hall of Fame:

1. The night nurse with the miner's hat who works in Cambridge House at the Big Hospital. He gets points for an unobtrusive manner, incredibly gentle technique and great hoop earrings.

2. The Dalai Lama look-alike. I loved him when he said, "Everyone has rolling veins; you just have to know what you are doing." And did he ever.

3. Any one of the techs from the lab across from the Costco in Waltham, Mass. They are reliably good. No one apologizes to anyone. They just take the blood and you're out of there in five minutes. They should get a huge bonus at holiday time.

My Lifetime Achievement Award, though, goes to Mock. Mock is a big Irish-American guy, a studly fellow who exudes confidence in a nice, reassuring way. He told me he went to nursing school back in the day when men were an oddity in those classrooms. Men his age and older made fun of him behind his back and to his face, calling him a name that questioned his virility.

Who's laughing now? You need to make an appointment six weeks in advance to get Mock to start your IV or grab a pint.

His graceful way with the needle and his easygoing, wicked hilarious attitude make him the most popular IV nurse at the Big Hospital.

24

Email Update:
Forth and Back

Hello, Everyone:

Andrea continues to improve. Most of her
levels are back to normal including her
white cell count, which is fantastic! She
is scheduled for a blood transfusion later
today in order to help her red cell count
get back to normal. Red blood cells regulate
energy level and once she receives new red
blood cells in the transfusion her energy
level will be greatly improved.

She will likely be transported back to the
Little Hospital tomorrow or the next day to
resume rehab. Today she has been permit-
ted to eat vanilla yogurt, toast and crack-
ers; not quite a Big Mac but certainly an
improvement from the broth.

I want to thank everyone who indicated they
would be able to visit Andrea's mother.
[Address.] I cannot emphasize enough how
much everyone's prayers, cards, flowers and
emails have meant to Andrea. I know that
visiting her mother Kay is a huge effort and
impossible for most of us because of distance, work, family, etc., but for those of
you who are able I just want you to know
what an enormous comfort it brings to Andrea
to know that people are able to spend some
time with her mother when she can't.

I think one of the greatest gifts throughout
this whole ordeal has been watching a community of people, many not knowing each other
but connected through our friendship with
Andrea, come together to contribute so much

love and support in such wonderfully personal and diverse ways. Hoping not to sound
trite, but the community that has gathered
around Andrea is really very powerful.

Alison

25

'You are so busted!'

One night I was at the Little Hospital for the second time. My friend Dave the Nurse was on duty. He was happy to see me and commented, "Your French manicure is really holding up." Now, who would notice?

He also pointed out which of the aides was a former hairdresser and suggested I ask her to do my hair. This had worked well at the Big Hospital. These are important quality-of-life issues that are scrutinized on patient satisfaction surveys.

A few days before I had broken out one of my caftans, this one from Hawaii dotted with a hibiscus print. For once I was abandoning my johnnie, probably for a special visitor.

Dave spotted me and said, "Look at you! All dressed up and your bedhead isn't as bad as usual!"

No higher praise.

I had no visitors one particular day. I was back in my johnnie and for the 100th time wondering why the beds had to be so back-breaking. I didn't feel like reading or writing in my journal. I was watching TV.

There was a news update about the disappearance of a woman and a small child from one of the southern states. They had showed up in New Hampshire and checked into a hotel. The mother was described as looking disheveled, unkempt and agitated. Another guest at the hotel heard yelling and a small child crying. After that night, he only saw the mother and she was gone a day or two later, alone. But where was the child?

Just because I was in the hospital, doesn't mean I was oblivious to current events. It wasn't all Lucy, Ethel and flipping wigs on the Jerry Springer show. Being a journalist was in my genes, and I had a social work degree, which means I might be a mandated reporter. Not usually when in the hospital myself, however. Whatever. I was unable to ignore what was going on.

Sadly, the small child's body had been discovered.

The only lead this particular afternoon was that a car matching the description of the mother's vehicle was spotted nearby. The child's mother was picked up for questioning. She was transported from the state police barracks to my Little Hospital for psychiatric evaluation.

I kept watching the news, waiting for more. The Little Hospital name was only mentioned once; after that it was referred to as "a nearby hospital." There weren't dozens to choose from. She and I were both being held in the same vicinity.

At this point I wasn't allowed to roam the halls at will; I needed permission. The fastest way to get information was to ring my co-conspirator. I immediately buzzed Dave. I asked him whether someone who was being evaluated would go to the ER or directly to the psych unit. He said the person would go to the ER, but why did I ask?

"Oh, I just saw something on TV about a woman being held and evaluated."

"Well, she's here. There are a bunch of state police cars out there," he said. At that point someone paged Dave on a legitimate patient care issue. I privately decided I had to get down there and check it out or I would never forgive myself.

A few minutes later he was back. I asked him if he would walk with me down to the little open area by elevators; I needed a change of scenery. He said he would, helping me with the IV pole. When we got there he pointed out the police cars down a few flights in the parking lot. I sat down in one of the chairs and told him I just wanted to hang out for a while.

As soon as he was out of sight, I got across to the elevator and punched the button for the emergency room. I don't know what I thought I would find. Maybe it would be a glimpse, some overheard conversation, a confession, a story of some kind. As I got off the elevator, the first thing I saw was a cop standing at the alert. The second thing was yellow police tape around the ER area.

I had my disguise – a johnnie, johnnie robe (a johnnie turned backwards) and skid-proof hospital socks. And my IV. I went right for the ER door and stopped there. I wasn't questioned.

I looked in the porthole of the door to see what I could see: Four or five uniformed police officers were in a semicircle around one of the ER curtained "rooms." The main ER door was locked, I knew. The only way I could get in closer was to ask for someone to buzz me in.

That far I couldn't go. I could look from 20 feet, through the small porthole window, but I had absolutely no real business being there. I waited long enough for one cop inside to turn around and look at me through the window, but not long enough for the one stationed at the elevator to consider me a security risk.

I made my way back, pulling my IV along and going back up on the elevator to my floor. I had to walk past the nurses' station to get back to my room. I knew I was in trouble, somehow, but what could they do? Fire me? From what? Court-martialed by the hospital military?

When I walked by, hoping to appear nonchalant, two nurses and the medical director rose as one: "Where have you been?"

"Downstairs," I said, and got back into bed.

"You are so busted!" I heard. That came from Dave, who had followed me into my room.

"Who do you think told them where I went?" I asked him, honestly mystified.

"I did."

Well, so much for my new BFF.

26

A what *pump?*

While my overall health seemed to be okay, weeks
after the surgery the massive Whipple/kidney incision was not healing. It could have been a nutritional
reason, too little protein, and that would have made
sense. I tried, but it had been hard to get down anything at all. Everything sounded unappetizing. Nothing tasted good.

It was almost as if someone said, "Here, have this
piece of tree bark. It's good for you."

This was what Dr. Whipple meant when he predicted
I would lose a lot of weight.

Maybe the gaping wound was due to too-early removal
of stitches, though I doubted that. My team at the
Big Hospital was convinced I was ready to have the

staples out; leaving them in too long would cause its own problems. No, I simply put it in the category of just dumb bad luck.

At that point I was "living" primarily at the Little Hospital rehab, shuttling back and forth to the Big Hospital in Boston when anything major happened. I was doing the Big Hospital-Little Hospital cha-cha-cha.

Dr. Whipple had been checking the incision at the Big Hospital and he wasn't happy with the lack of healing. At one point sent me back to the Little Hospital rehab with orders for a vacuum wound pump, whatever that was. It sounded hideous, but I assumed I would stay at the rehab and the nurses would take care of it. I assumed wrong. They "weren't trained" on the wound pump, I was told. Nobody on the unit was.

"Nobody?" I asked.

Nobody.

"So where will I go with my traveling pump?"

Home.

Home? As in the place where I can barely operate my own thermostat?

It sounded like a high-tech medieval torture machine. What would be next, the rack?

It turns out a wound pump is similar to a canister vacuum cleaner. It has a tube that goes into the wound, in the vicinity of my midsection, with foam blocks of various sizes all around it to keep it in place.

The tube is then taped down with clear packaging tape. The tube runs from the patient to a machine that looks like a large LED clock radio and pumps whatever it pulls out into a Plexiglas box. The box snaps into the side of the machine and is emptied and measured by a visiting nurse every day. It comes with a canvas carrying case with a strap and weighs what seems like about 10 pounds, though it must be less.

This is all well and good, but I was terrified at the idea of being alone with the vacuum pump, watching it pump my insides into the clear plastic box. I was told that it would emit a buzzing when it was doing its job, which was 24/7.

Of course I assumed "buzz" to be "roar," much as a dentist describes excruciating pain as "some discomfort." How could I even sleep?

If there was a problem, it would stop buzzing and start beeping, my signal to call an 800 number for further instructions.

And I would have to leave the hospital immediately. Once there, a visiting nurse would show me how to operate it because no one in the hospital had the expertise.

In an absolute blind panic, I threw myself on the mercy of my dear friend Linda. She is a retired nurse, having worked in both psych and hospice (couldn't be more perfect). Even better, she was a good friend and good sport. I asked her if I could go home with her for a few days and stay at her house. The visiting nurse could see me there, and Linda knew her way around wound pumps.

She was fine with it. So was her sainted husband. I'm sure I was all they needed, as they were in the final stages of demolition of their kitchen. Maybe the sound of cabinets being ripped off the walls would drown out the sound of my new appendage.

At that point I stopped hyperventilating and relaxed.

Linda picked me up at the hospital. On the way from the Little Hospital to her house, she offered to stop to visit my mother Kay, AKA Nuzzie. I hadn't seen her in the weeks since the Whipple. She seemed happy to see me, was her sparkly, cheerful self and didn't ask me where I had been (a little odd). I was incredibly relieved to see her. She looked good.

We sat on the little enclosed porch and talked. Nuzzie seemed contented and calm. I had been talking to the caretakers, nurses and my friend the chaplain on the phone. My mom was doing fine physically with no doctor visits and on her scaled-back medication regime. She was now down to just thyroid replacement and a blood thinner from her extensive laundry list of medicines.

She had perked up so much since getting there that the staff could hardly keep up with her. She had trouble walking and didn't know her limitations, so she had been getting out of bed and stumbling around the room. On one occasion they found her sitting in a chair across the room, legs crossed, acting as if nothing were amiss. Even with monitoring her on closed-circuit TV, they couldn't get there in time. She was *fast*. But she hadn't fallen yet.

"I don't know where everybody is," she said. It was true, most people were bedridden. She was sprightly by comparison. (This was reminiscent to me of the time everyone cleared out of the Big Hospital to go to the Outback Steakhouse. There were more than a few parallels.)

What my mother needed was mental stimulation. Always social, she now craved nonstop company. She was forgetful and a little confused, but that was okay, it didn't seem to frustrate her.

My short visit to the hospice lacked any kind of drama, thankfully. I felt guilty about her being there, and hoped they could keep her from hopping out of bed and getting hurt. I would settle for safe. It was the best I could do.

I felt a mixture of sadness and relief leaving her that day. I told one of the nurses I thought she seemed really good. They agreed, but one nurse looked at me and said, "*You* don't look all that great, though." She got credit for honesty.

I was privately hoping I could get back to celebrate my mom's 91st birthday in a few weeks.

But Linda took me home with her, to the place where I would be for what would turn out to be a full week. It had been a big day for me, and after the longish car ride I was exhausted physically and emotionally. The guest room was a glorious luxury oasis of soft, puffy comforters and pillows.

Linda and her husband, Gabe, were excellent company. They introduced me to reruns of "Doc Martin," the PBS series about the surgeon who suddenly develops a fear of blood and leaves his London practice to become a country practitioner in Cornwall. Just my speed.

The next day the visiting nurse came and installed the pump. When the pump whirred on, the suction grabbed me. I hadn't jumped that high since the therapy dog bit me. But it relaxed its grip, and so did I. The machine proved to be quiet. It was indeed more of a purr. And after the initial shock of suction, it was okay.

I slept like a baby until 3 a.m. that first night, when my machine turned off and the beeping began. I could have awakened Linda, but I dialed the 800 number and was told to turn it off and reset it. I did, and went back to sleep.

Apparently the machine would turn off now and then, and I could usually get it back on track by punching myself in the midsection to maneuver the tube into alignment and get it going again.

Eventually, I left the safety of my lovely room. I packed up my pump and, with some trepidation, got ready to go home.

27

Email Update:
Tobin Girls

Hello, everyone:

Andrea has been sprung from the clink…um, I mean rehab. She is staying in an undisclosed location for a few days so that she can be assisted with her last drain and over-all recuperation. She is not sure when she will be back in her house, but probably next week. Andrea had the opportunity to go visit her mother yesterday and was relieved to find her in much better health than she was a month ago. The motto here is: Never underes-timate a Tobin Girl!

Andrea will be getting a vacuum pump to help aid in the healing of the wound. Also, she said she would be thrilled to have some company in the mornings or afternoons next week to keep her laughing and help her with getting around. She is strong and able to walk but lifting more than 5 lbs. is still a challenge. I'm sure she will have plenty of eager volunteers.

Well, I think we can all let out a sigh of relief!

Thanks,

Alison

28

Wound down

Once back in my own house, I didn't go out much. I was happy to hang out with my dog, read, and sleep. The wound pump hum was a sort of white noise and it put me to sleep, although there usually wasn't a problem. I was becoming an Olympic-caliber napper.

My friends were used to seeing me at my absolute worst. But dressing for more than a trip to the kitchen called for creativity, which I got good at. I wore dresses with a pocket, cut a hole in the pocket and ran the tube in. The tube was attached to this machine. I usually wore a raincoat over the whole clunky apparatus. So what if I looked like a flasher?

When I was home, the visiting nurses came every day or two to empty the receptacle (I averted my eyes) and measured the incision opening. The numbers were not impressive.

I never actually saw my own incision. I didn't want to, and I avoided spending time in front of a full-length mirror. The non-healing incision led me to make a whole new batch of friends at the outpatient Wound Clinic at the Big Hospital. I found people to drive me downtown a couple of times, for them to check it, but still not much was happening. It just wasn't closing up.

Dr. Whipple was extremely unhappy with the lack of progress. The third time I was there he came into the examining room in the Wound Clinic, hacked away at the excess tissue at the incision site, which is actually a crude description of what is called *debridement*. My poor friend Cindy was in a prime spot to see him work on it, and she looked extremely queasy. She said she was fine; she is not a good liar.

Dr. Whipple replaced the wound pump and powered it on.

"It won't take long now, maybe only two or three weeks."

Two or three *more weeks? Only? Are you kidding me?*

But what could I do? I lived with it. If I had learned anything, it was that you can get used to almost anything.

I was constantly reminded that things could be a lot worse. Who wants to be reminded of that? But it was true. Everyone kept telling me what a good patient I was, so I would continue to try to live up to that.

In the end, I see Dr. Whipple's vigorous trimming as a turning point. The parade of visiting nurses kept coming to measure; it was clearly healing. He was right about the healing time. In just about three weeks, it was removed. Amazing as it sounds, I am now a big fan of the wound pump.

I would do infomercials, but I think women are more interested in creams that will slow the march of time across their faces.

29

Heckuva gingerbread man and Alien Baby

It had been nine months since the April surgery, and there were plumbing problems, fevers, infections, stent changes one after the other, and technology malfunctions. My magnesium was up, my potassium was down. Or maybe it was the other way around. My body felt like a fixer-upper.

Everyone said the same thing. "We have to be careful. You only have one kidney. *Actually, you only have a piece of one kidney.*" It was true, and they were careful with me.

It had been well over a year since I had been to Ireland and I idly wondered if and when I would get back. Francis and I were no longer in contact, but I had other friends there and a strong connection.

In the current hierarchy of needs, though, returning to Ireland was not on the radar. I would, in fact, have been scared to death to travel anywhere at that point.

Things were not terrible, but I was just getting sick of my new and unpredictable normal. I had lost a lot of weight since the "reorganization," as I liked to call it. I was thin but my addomen was lumpy and still numb.

After Christmas something new and disturbing had appeared on the landscape.

I didn't know exactly what was going on, but if I had to guess, the answer would have been "fat."

The thing kept growing. It was bigger this week than last. I didn't really know where my stomach was, and wasn't part of it removed anyway? That made self-diagnosis beyond the realm of my Internet-based medical knowledge grab-bag.

In January, I went to my primary care physician to get her opinion.

"It's an incisional hernia," she said, upon inspection. "I think you should get it checked out if you're concerned."

Would it get bigger?

"Oh, yes."

If I was concerned? How long would it take for me to be concerned? When it was the size of a mango, a pineapple, or a watermelon? Would I wait until I couldn't compare it to any kind of fruit? When I couldn't get through a doorway sideways or have to insist on two seats in the bulkhead of a plane? I was definitely too long in the tooth to pass for being pregnant.

I went home and got on my laptop to search hernia repair persons. There on the Big Hospital website in living color was a photo of my surgeon, Dr. Whipple himself, with hat, scrubs and mask. I called for an appointment to see him.

But first I found out a few things. My bump did resemble the incisional hernia, a gift of the surgery that keeps on giving... trouble. It isn't a rare occurrence, even though 10 months had gone by. I wasn't special. I didn't want to be special. I wanted to be ordinary. And just when I was beginning to hope I could glimpse the light at the end of the tunnel.

I went to my appointment with Dr. Whipple. By this time, my bump resembled a third breast.

I took my friend Sharon with me to the appointment, because I knew from experience you never know when simple things will become complicated and, boom, there you are in the emergency room. After taking a look, Dr. Pancreas/Whipple-now-Dr. Hernia repeated what my primary care doc had said, that it was an incisional hernia.

I told him I had previously self-diagnosed it as an over-abundance of Christmas cookies.

"That would be one heckuva gingerbread man!" he said, laughing.

This doctor also acted as if it were elective surgery. Did I want to have the repair? Am I just vain? It seemed like a no-brainer decision to me.

But maybe it was an insurance issue. At the rate it was growing, I thought there was no time to waste.

So I asked the question: "Is this considered cosmetic?"

Dr. Hernia started smiling. He must have been reading my mind. "No, and insurance covers it."

I asked if it could be repaired by laparoscopy. (I had read on the Internet that it could.)

"Oh, no, not in your case, you have to have open surgery."

OK, maybe that is one reason doctors tell you not to go to the Internet. It just stirs up envy of everyone else who can have laparoscopy. I have never had a single procedure done through laparoscopy, and I'm always told that it is on a case-to-case basis, depending on a lot of factors. Intellectually I understood it, but still wanted to throw myself on the floor in a temper tantrum right then and there.

He said he would use a mesh of some kind, probably Gore-Tex – nice for Massachusetts winters, I thought.

I asked Sharon if she could think of any questions for the doctor. Just one, as it turned out. "Can I have one, too?"

A couple of weeks later, at the suggestion of one of my doctors who detected a certain frustration on my part, I joined a cancer survivor support group. I privately thought of us as on the spectrum of Bereaved, Relieved, Peeved. I know we were all, naturally, thrilled to be in the "survivor" column, but frayed by the process and worried about upcoming follow-ups.

The group members varied vastly in age, but all were supportive, nice people, though at very different places in their process. One man had had cancer seven years before and hardly remembered it. We labeled him lucky, and so did he. One of the women got lunch through a tube in her abdomen and was so genuinely matter-of-fact about it and positive that she inspired the rest of us to get on with it and stop whining.

One person said she told everyone she knew when she got cancer and felt blamed; she received a lot of hurtful advice suggesting she could have avoided it by eating differently. How about choosing parents more carefully? Please.

One woman said all her friends told her she should write a book about her cancer experience. The group facilitator and I had previously discussed my writing this book; she and I didn't make eye contact.

Another woman hadn't told anyone at work she had cancer because she was afraid it would hurt her professionally if she was seen as sick. There were examples she could point to where this very thing had happened in her company. So she went through che-motherapy and radiation, making excuses all the way along. The stress of the cover-up seemed an extraordi-narily cruel punishment on top of already coping with the seriousness of the disease.

Of the people in the support group, Maureen was the only other member of the Whipple club. It is an elite organization, something like an Ivy League college with cheaper tuition. Still, it is surprising how many of us there are. When I find one, like the man who lives a few blocks from me, we often find out we share the same surgeon. Dr. Pancreas/Whipple. performs more than150 per year, so I guess it isn't shocking. But I like the synchronicity.

I must have been bragging to Maureen that I was going to have an incisional hernia repair. Not that she was competitive, but she said she thought she might have a hernia, too. She wanted to see mine. I didn't exactly bare my belly, but cradled it as a pregnant woman would her bump. She showed me hers – it was smaller, but they were sisters as bumps go.

She told me that her bump was quite obvious to members of her exercise class, who had named it Alien Baby.

Maureen hadn't thought about seeking medical attention by an obstetrician, but immediately went to her oncologist and, yes, she had an incisional hernia. And she, too, had a choice as to whether to get it repaired. She decided to punt. So there are people who choose to wait and see what happens.

The support group finished its prescribed eight weeks and we went our separate ways. I had a date for my own hernia repair and was anxious to get it over with.

I never heard about Alien Baby again.

Without surgery would it be the size of a toddler by now?

30

Losing it

As the one-year anniversary of the Whipple came around, the cancer scans again were still coming up clear.

When there is cancer surgery, the oncologist takes a back seat and the surgeon drives. At this point I was assigned to a new, and pretty fantastic, oncologist. When Dr. Oncology suggested seeing a social worker in his department for a few non-physical kinks in the works, I wasn't sure that he was right, especially since he was recommending a man. I was totally wrong, and grateful to Dr. Oncology for suggesting someone who turned out to be perfect for me.

There had been bouts of anemia, so I was eating baby spinach by the barrel and had blood transfusions. A nutritionist was consulted, another service of the Big Hospital. My potassium and magnesium numbers were regulated back to normal.

At this point my iron level was almost back to normal and I had gained back five to 10 of the 50 pounds lost in the last year. I was still closely monitored, and took my temperature twice a day. If it was high to the slightest degree, I was instructed to go directly to the hospital, which I did, as frustrated as I was to keep going back there.

My own Alien Baby hernia was repaired by my good friend, Dr. Whipple. It was a blissfully simple procedure with an easy recovery.

The stent connecting my bladder and kidney made me feel in a constant state of "yucky" and I almost never made it to the suggested every-three-month replacement schedule before there was some problem that sent me back to interventional radiology. I had recurrent urinary tract infections and the stent was an irritating, annoying, uncomfortable presence.

It was usually my choice of conscious sedation or general anesthesia for the stent replacement procedure and I always opted for the latter. I had no interest in sharing the experience in any conscious way. I was getting to know people in the interventional radiology department and in the recovery room. Sometimes I was admitted to the hospital overnight, but typically went home at the end of the day.

 A couple of weeks after the hernia repair, the quarterly stent replacement was due, so I had an appointment with Dr. Kidney. The second appointment that day was with Dr. Whipple to take the 12 stitches out of the hernia incision, and then there was still time for the intake procedure for the stent replacement after that.

At any rate, when I went to see Dr. Kidney about the upcoming stent replacement, he wanted to see the hernia site. He couldn't restrain himself, I guess, and clipped out the staples Dr. Whipple had put in.

"I'm going to make Dr. Whipple's day," he said, grinning. When I got to Dr. Whipple's office, he was understandably mystified to see that the staples were gone. Now he might have thought he owed Dr. Kidney a favor. As far as I was concerned, it was great to get rid of all that metal. I didn't care who got the blame or credit.

Two days later, the stent replacement went smoothly. Mary drove me in and then home. She did not shy from standing up for me to get the best care. This time she didn't have to rough up any of the members of the interventional radiation staff to get what she determined was the right treatment for me.

On the family front, my San Francisco daughter was now engaged and we were all delighted. She and her fiancé were planning a September wedding in the Boston area.

My mother, Nuzzie, had been restless in the residential hospice and was confused and sometimes delusional. A few months before, the hospice director recommended I move her into an Alzheimer's unit.

My friend Nancy, my son and few others, including my brother and sister-in-law who flew in from Chicago, helped move her belongings from one place to another.

Both my kids visited their grandmother whenever they were in town, and though Nuzzie was losing ground cognitively she was always happy to see them. She was thrilled to see her granddaughter try on her wedding gown.

My mother used to tell me that I should enjoy the little things in life, because big things didn't come around very often. In earlier days, it could be staying up all night reading a great book, especially if my dad was out of town. These days it was socks, she never got tired of colorful socks and it was easy to make her happy by bringing her a new pair with stripes or wild patterns.

Now, though, at the end of March, Nuzzie was having a series of small strokes and was suffering from increasingly more severe congestive heart failure. There continued to be many close calls. She was also losing names.

"Who's that?" an aide asked my mother when I arrived one afternoon.

"That's my daughter," Nuzzie said.

"What's her name?"

She thought a minute. "Beautiful lady."

She remembered golfers. In fact, she told the staff one day that same week that she had been married to Tiger Woods.

Would that make Tiger my dad?

31

Easter morning

At Eastertime about a year after the Whipple, I
was invited to my mother's Alzheimer's unit Easter
celebration. Credit to the staff, they celebrated every
holiday: religious, secular, pagan, you name it. A luau
in the summer, St. Patrick's Day, 4th of July, Martin
Luther King Day, Valentine's Day.

This occasion was no exception. The snacks were
plentiful: chocolate eggs, Peeps, M&M's. Decorations
included banners, signs, garlands, candy baskets,
blow-up bunnies in Easter bonnets, fluffy stuffed baby
chicks. Best of all, much of the staff wore costumes.
I thought one aide couldn't top her light-up elf getup
from Christmas, but I was wrong.

The Easter party fell on my birthday, so when the gui-
tar player was taking requests I asked for a "Happy

Birthday," then, the Beatles' song "When I'm 64," which was my private joke, since that was my 64th. I'm not sure Nuzzie caught the lyrics, but she clapped along and got in the spirit of the music.

My mom asked for and received a double portion of ice cream before lunch that day, and snatched the almost-empty bowl back when an aide tried to take it away to make room for the healthy meal that was coming. No one went hungry at the Easter party.

Late the next night, Good Friday, I was awakened by the phone ringing. It was a nurse at my mother's Alzheimer's unit saying Nuzzie was being rushed to the hospital.

"She's having a really hard time breathing. There is an aide with her, but I think you should go over there right away," he said.

Another emergency room! As I walked down my back steps to the car, the church bells on the Common were chiming three.

When I arrived at the hospital my mother was sleeping. The aide from the Alzheimer's unit was still there with her, I was glad to see.

There had been plenty of emergency room visits, despite a living will that might have avoided them if held to documentation. She also had a DNR. One of the emergency room nurses took me aside and questioned me very closely about my mother's wishes regarding comfort-only treatment. And then the doctor talked with me about it.

It was clear to me what my mother would have chosen, as much as she had loved her life. It felt like the right time to stop heroic measures.

Nuzzie was moved to a private room with a table set up with bottled water and leftover Passover cookies. I spent the day with her and she slipped out of consciousness. We sat together, I talked and to this day choose to believe she heard me. I got into bed with her. Every now and then she would sit up, open her eyes and then fall back, asleep.

My brother had already arranged to come in from Chicago for Easter, so he drove directly to the hospital from the airport that afternoon.

We were in the hospital with our mother when she died peacefully in the early hours of Easter morning. She was almost 92. Our dad had died almost 20 years before. It was shocking to lose her. It was a gentle passing, but still hard to believe.

There were a few papers to sign. The hospital staff was respectful and kind. It was like falling out of a plane in slow motion. My world had always had my mother in it.

My brother Chris and I got back to my house at 7:30 in the morning, and we didn't know what to do with ourselves, so we went to my church. No Protestant church would consider Easter truly Easter without the hymn, "Christ the Lord is Risen Today." My brother and I knew the melody from our childhood in the Congregational Church. First Parish (Unitarian) has different, gender-inclusive lyrics. "Lo, the Earth Awakes Again" were just different words to a familiar, very comforting song. The phrase, "spring and gladness are before" seemed a celebration.

It was a privilege to be able to go to my church home of 30 years and light a candle for my mother just hours after her passing, and get a few hugs afterwards that day.

A few weeks later there was a memorial service for my mother at First Parish. My son, my daughter and her fiancé and my brother and sister-in-law were there, I was so thankful to have our whole small family together. The minister John, who had sat at her hospital bedside a year before when we thought she wouldn't survive the night, did a wonderful, highly individual and meaningful service.

There were songs from the '40s by Gabe and his ensemble; "Amazing Grace" on the bagpipes by our good friend Joanne; and a recording of Andrea Bocelli's "My Prayer" which Nuzzie and I had heard live in concert with the Boston Pops.

Nuzzie would have loved it.

32

Being carried

The small group of volunteers that assembled leading up to the Whipple had come together into a stalwart little army that hung in together when the months turned into a year and beyond.

It's one step to accept help, another leap to dare to ask for it. People aren't mind-readers.

When my mother died, the volunteer who organized the memorial services at my church said, "When people ask you what they can do, suggest they bring flowers from their gardens."

I did, and they did, and it was such a nice thing. It was Memorial Day weekend, so the homegrown flowers were in their springtime prime.

My own garden benefited from the goodwill all the way along.

Polly's son Carl did a major yard cleanup early that summer. He did the best job ever, and I didn't even know it was happening until he left.

Cindy spent three hours tearing a tenacious vine out of my rhododendron bush at the corner of my front yard.

She came in sweating and said, "Have you ever thought of moving to a condominium?" I said no, why should I as long as I could get so many volunteers to take care of my house?

Judy planted perennials, Mary ripped pesky grass out of the garden in front of the picket fence, and Marlene filled window boxes lush with lantana, coleus, and annuals I couldn't even name.

Other people ran errands, bought pajamas, cooked for me when nothing tasted good, and stayed overnight if things seemed dicey (I actually had a bell to summon help).

For a long time I slept in a tiny den with a TV off the living room, close to kitchen and a tiny bathroom. People stopped by, some who didn't know each other previously became friends.

There was a feeling of camaraderie that was incredibly comforting, and occasionally a few skirmishes over who would do what. But just hearing people talking and laughing in the other room made me feel safe. I could drift off to sleep or not.

Could I have anticipated any of this? Not in a million years. Neither my own long months of neediness nor the staggering generosity of people.

For months I would get better, something would happen, and no sooner would I get over that, that another glitch appeared. Many events fell into the silly or ridiculous category, some not so much. The unpredictability was the only predictable aspect. Looking back, I had some kind of emergency hospital visit at least every month.

It not a true war against cancer, since I was cancer-free after the surgery but more of a reconstruction of the battlefield. It was similar to a road trip that went on too long, actually, till everyone was ready to ask the question: "Why didn't we fly?"

Speaking of road trips, early on in the recovery period, one rainy Sunday morning, I asked my neighbor Phyllis if she would drive me the few blocks to our neighborhood drugstore to pick up a couple of things.

Phyllis always, always, always looks bohemian chic. But she isn't judgmental about what anyone else wears. It's a good thing, or she wouldn't have been seen in public with me that day.

At that time in my life, I had a collection of caftans, typically worn with a T-shirt underneath. It always made me laugh when people complimented me on one of those ensembles. Come to think of it, the compliments typically came from people who were used to seeing me in a johnnie.

My clothing at that time was selected by the degree of grace with which it could disguise what was underneath. I don't remember what the tube count was that day, probably just a couple.

(At one point in the hospital I had seven drains with bags, often referred to by the nurses as "big boys" or "bad boys," depending on the size, whether it was closer to an envelope or a hand grenade. "Boy" was the common denominator designation with the female nurses.)

It was a quick errand that morning, nothing extraordinary about it, but Phyllis and I were both in high spirits. We picked up a few things, checked out, and proceeded to the parking lot.

Lowering myself into Phyllis's car, I gathered up the voluminous skirt and we took off.

After a couple of minutes I looked down and saw that the car door had slammed on one of the tubes, trapping the bag on the outside of the car.

"Uh-oh. One of my tubes is outside the door."

Phyllis quickly pulled over, and I opened the door and reeled it back in. The balloon-shaped bag that should have been attached to the tube was missing. I could only guess it was still at CVS.

"Oh my God. The bag is gone."

In retrospect, this was good; better than dragging on the ground, though the tube was already leaking into the floor of Phyllis's car.

"Don't worry, we'll go right back," she said.

She turned around in a driveway. I was hoping it wasn't in the crowded store somewhere, as in "Pardon me, sir, you're standing on something squishy that doesn't belong to you."

We drove right back and luckily, despite the wind-shield wipers, Phyllis spotted it right away. There it was, a bomb-like object in a rain puddle on the pavement of the parking lot. Phyllis jumped right out to retrieve it.

"No!" I said. "Don't – it's disgusting."

"I'm a doctor's wife, this is nothing. I'll grab it."

And before you could say "Bob's your uncle," she had splashed through the parking and, still laughing, picked up the bag and handed it to me.

For some reason, this misadventure put us into even better humor. There was something exhilarating about the utter absurdity of the situation.

Absurdity was a frequent state.

33

Bye, stent

My good friend was with me on one of my frequent trips to Dr. Kidney's office, a beautiful summer day to drive into Boston. We ended up having an unusually long wait.

It was to be a painful but blessedly quick procedure.

There is no doctor I like better than my kidney surgeon. I have lots of company in that respect. Whenever I mention him downtown, I hear, "Dr. Kidney, he's wonderful," or "You have the best urology surgeon in this hospital." He's a great guy, and at this point had been with me through kidney cancer three times.

Beyond that, though, as a single woman of a certain age, there is no more promising place to meet men of my age group than a urologist's office. I am almost always the only woman in there.

If a man in the waiting room has a woman next to him, it's obvious they are a couple. She is the one in the adjoining chair who nudges him and says, "She just called your name" because her hearing – corrected by a hearing aid that she was actually willing to get when she became deaf – is better than his.

But if there isn't a woman in the next chair, the man is probably available and fun to talk to. By "fun," I mean along the lines of, "Do you know if we leave the little cups in the bathroom or bring them back to the desk?" Scintillating conversation like that.

That is the good news. There is nearly always a nice-looking 60-or 70-something with a full head of gray hair or at least no comb-over.

The bad news, of course, is that about 99 percent of these men have a male-only variety of cancer, and we all know what that means. Looking ahead, it would probably be a brother-sister relationship or better living through chemistry. But I digress. That's what happens when there aren't enough new magazines in the waiting room and that architectural design book from 1967 doesn't warrant more than three or four readings.

I thought the hard part about the Whipple/kidney surgery would be complications from the Whipple. I was warned there could be several; it was to be a tough recovery in anyone's opinion. But it turned out my life was not a living hell, but a consistent pain. I blame the kidney, okay, *a part of one kidney*, since that was all I had left. If it wasn't one thing, it was another. The trouble is, it was always something to do with that one thing.

I was in the office that day to rid myself of something I had never seen but knew much too intimately: a ureteral stent. It was the tube that hooked into the kidney, ran through the ureter, and then attached with the same pigtail loop to the bladder. The kidney hematoma eruption months and months before had damaged the pathway.

According to the literature, *many* to *most* patients are aware of the stent *much* or *most* of the time. That is not a good thing. Awareness is one thing, constant irritation and pain another, but my experience was that it was all three.

Other side effects I read about were encrustation (nope), fragmentation (also negative), migration into other parts of the body (not that I knew of, thank God), increased urinary frequency (very much so), or incontinence (occasionally). I never actually laid eyes on the stent or its many predecessors till it came out for the very last time that day.

The stent was supposed to be changed every three months unless things went wrong, and they had gone wrong frequently. It was installed in July after the April Whipple and was changed as frequently as two weeks after the last one, each requiring a trip to interventional radiology and a journey into the never-never land of anesthesia.

It had been trouble, trouble, trouble, resulting in aches and nonstop urinary tract infections. I was finally getting it out, more than a year later, and Dr. Kidney was literally taking a new direction this time. There was already the nephrostomy tube, a back-up that allowed me to urinate out my back and bypass the bathroom. This could be a middle-aged woman's dream: No getting up in the middle of the night, at least not for that reason.

My friend offered to come in and hold my hand but I said I was okay, I could tough it out.

I changed my mind as soon as I went inside and motioned for her to join me.

This friend always made me laugh, still makes me laugh. She did not disappoint that day, standing at my head and whispering inappropriate things in my ear. She made fun of my red gingham checked bikini underpants, saying they looked like something Rebecca of Sunnybrook Farm would wear.

But I wasn't laughing when the surgeon got out what looked like a fishing rod to grab the stent. Using the rod somehow -- I had my eyes closed – he fished it out. It was quick and painless, once it done. When I looked at it I was surprised how thin it actually was and so long, at least 10 inches. I had pictured the stent differently, more like the tubes we play with as kids made of woven straw that we would put one finger in and our friend put her finger in and try to get them out.

This skinny little thing had been the cause of such misery? I was ecstatic, though.

What came next couldn't be as bad. What an optimist. Well, maybe different, if not as bad.

Still using his trusty fishing rod, he tossed it into the trash.

Dr. Kidney left the room, but his nurse was still there. "Does anyone ever save these?" I asked her.

"Sometimes. One man put his on his Christmas tree," she said.

My friend was horrified; she looked at me, looking slightly nauseous. "If you do that, I'm *never* coming over!"

She moved to Florida after that. I don't think it had anything to do with my Christmas tree.

34

Photo shoot on the deck

Counting my blessings became a mantra: no new
cancer, no chemotherapy, no radiation, no dialysis,
no diabetes, an amazing group of entertaining people
around me, first-class medical care, no sustained pain.

Still, starting from the very beginning of this process,
once I was out of the Whipple/kidney operating room,
I had one eye on the various drains and tubes that
were running in and out of me, not exactly like well-
oiled, though often oily, machines.

Once home, there were various visiting nurses over
the months, and, with a few (outrageous) exceptions,
they were good at what they did. Insurance sometimes
dictated what a patient needed, i.e. would cover.

My doctor wanted the nephrostomy tube that connected my kidney through my back and out flushed

(cleaned) every day. This operation required skill with a stopcock, which none of the rest of us here in my little posse had ever heard of. (It was a valve on the tube controlling the flow.)

A visiting nurse could come twice, at times three, times a week. I could not physically reach around my back and do it myself. Somebody had to use the stopcock.

One of my friends, probably the most squeamish of all of us, volunteered to have the nurse teach her how to do it. (We raised our kids together; when we had to rush off to the ER for a childhood accident, I drove while she screamed.) Trust me when I say it was a major challenge; it scared the socks off her.

"I'm so afraid I'm going to kill you," she told me the first time. But she learned it, got used to doing it and came over two or three times a week until we got the go-ahead from the doctor to ease up the schedule.

One day I was having trouble yet again with a tube. The nephrostomy tube connection was the problem. It had a dressing where the tube exited my back with a dressing around it and what looked like a CD over it. It wasn't the tube itself, it was my skin where the device was attached: it itched like crazy. I wanted to rub my back against the nearest pine tree and give it a good scratch. (Pine sap would definitely not be an effective all-natural remedy.)

Then the area quickly developed a weeping rash that made me feel like crying. I called Dr. Kidney's office to be told what to do. Bear in mind, his office was in the city, more than an hour's drive from where I lived. He had a room of men waiting to see him, and we didn't know if I should drive in or not.

I had already read my instructions on when to call the doctor, including redness at the site, new swelling or drainage at the site, broken stitches, yada, yada, yada.

Some of these conditions were on the checklist, but Dr. Kidney clearly needed a visual. I couldn't get a very good look at it. Where he was located 20 miles away, he couldn't see it at all.

His nurse was trying to get a handle on the situation. I asked her if she had a smart phone. Yes, she did.

Me: "May I send you a picture of it?"

"To my personal cell phone?"

Me: "Yes."

"Well...okay."

Natural light is always desirable, so I went out on my back deck, pulled up my shirt and tried to take a picture of what can safely be described as an awkward place.

Think of the intersection of your spine and waist. (If you are a young woman you might have what is called a tramp stamp right there.) Imagine your back as a map of the United States. The spot where your waist and backbone come meet is New Orleans.

Go northeast from New Orleans and the tube would be at approximately Tuscaloosa, Alabama. Take Route 10 to 59 to 20. It's probably easier to drive from New Orleans to Tuscaloosa than take a picture of your own back.

I tried to do it myself, meaning take the picture with my phone, not drive. I had to hold up my shirt with one hand. (I wasn't going topless for this, not with a partial view from the street.) Then I attempted to wedge the phone between the disc holding the tube and my skin. The phone had to be far enough from the "subject" to focus. It just wasn't happening. The nurse wasn't on hold, but she was waiting.

Phyllis was summoned from her house across the street. This is a good friend. She didn't ask why or when. She knew it was now, and she knew she would do whatever.

Would she mind taking a picture of my back? Not at all. Between the two of us, we accomplished this task. It took all four hands. Yep, it was totally disgusting. One of the things I love about Phyllis is that she takes things in stride.

She said something diplomatic, like, "It looks sore."

My doctor, it turned out, couldn't tell much from the cell phone photo either. He told me I'd better come in. So I went downtown.

My friends in the Big Hospital interventional radiology department were waiting for me. They cleaned up the area and replaced the metal CD-like disc with a brand-new attachment that looked more like a box that would fit on the head of a travel toothbrush.

It was tasteful, tiny, and shiny clean.

Suddenly there was the distinct sound of my back heaving a sigh of relief.

35

Yeast: Not your grandmother's ingredient

Although almost totally unproductive in any usual sense, not contributing to the GNP, I began to realize I needed to be gentle with myself and patient with the inevitable setbacks in the healing process. I was coming out of the woods, interested in eating again, getting more energy.

A new problem was on the rise, however.

One afternoon I started feeling lousy in general, and pretty soon was so cold I was shaking under the blankets. The house wasn't cold. It must be me, I thought. I wanted to stay warm under the covers and make the whole thing go away.

Watching the temperature climb on my thermometer, when the fever reached 102 I knew where I was headed. I had just won another trip to the emergency room and was not happy.

That day my friend Molly had stopped by to visit and I admitted I had the teeniest smidgen of a fever. I did not want to go yet again. She insisted. I was furious with her (she reminded me later).

But Molly was right for holding firm on that one. She called for the ambulance and I was admitted immediately upon my arrival at the Big Hospital.

That night my temperature spiked to 106. I was glad I was in the hospital, taken care of and packed in ice instead of sweating it out in front of my TV at home – or worse.

The diagnosis astounded me: I had a yeast infection.

This particular brand of yeast infection had everyone running. My doctor was fearing that the infection had spread to my heart, so I had an echocardiogram. That was a foreign procedure for me. It hurt like hell. I felt like my chest was the mortar and the technician held the pestle and she was grinding away for literally more than an hour. Luckily there was no indication of cardiac yeast from the kidney.

Then they were worried about my eyes. Was there yeast there?

"When you get through with the echocardiogram you will have to go to the eye and ear clinic, but first get cleared through their own emergency department," I was told. Great.

When I got back to my hospital room after the echo, a surprise was waiting for me: a woman in a white lab coat with a lantern strapped to her head. Yes, doctors do make house calls. This ophthalmologist was there to check my eyes for yeast. It took a blink of an eye. None!

A happy dance was in order. Cross "blind" off the list of concerns.

There were a few days in the hospital, then back home, where I could wear dowager queen caftans to hide the outdoor plumbing. Not only that, I could eat anything, hell, everything, and no one would ever know. It took me back to the wound pump days.

This tube was attached to my clothing, secured with an assortment of huge pins. Just try to find diaper pins when everyone is using Pampers.

The tube would have to be replaced periodically, just like the stent before it. This also meant a trip to the interventional radiology department. If it shifted, which it could, that would mean the tube would have to be taken out and repositioned even more often.

There were other downsides. No matter how clean I was, I worried about residual odor. My medical supply company sent me boxes of receptacle bags that were covered by my medical insurance but I was ordering extra ones at my own expense. (Worth it.) Sometimes some part of the apparatus would rip and I kept extra clothes in my car, even in my purse. At night there could be more problems.

One result of all of these things was that I was afraid to be out of range of the Big Hospital because I had an irrational fear bordering on the rational that anything could happen. Speaking of that, more than one doctor was sympathetic about what invariably was referred to as my "saga." From my perspective, I got good care.

Good thing for me, by accident of birth I was living in the 21st century and cared for in an excellent medical institution. If it were a few dozen decades earlier, I might have been crossing the continent in a covered wagon. Of course, if I had lived in Boston I could have said no to the Gold Rush and gone to this very same hospital.

I also contracted MRSA. Remember MRSA? I tested positive for methicillin-resistant *staphylococcus aureus* at one point, which meant that for months everyone had to gown up and take precautions to come in contact with me. That didn't end until I had three consecutive negative readings on that particular stubborn bacteria. There was some grumbling about that and it wasn't coming from me. MRSA was the least of my worries, and eventually I had the all-clear, but while it lasted it was cumbersome for everyone who had to treat me.

After the nephrostomy tube was in for a few months, I was getting discouraged. The device on my back that irritated my skin was gone, replaced by the smaller snap-open box. Better, much better, but still uncomfortable.

I wasn't depressed, but I was getting worn down, still running back and forth to the hospital with fevers and infections and replacements. It was hard to take a shower, "just wrap Saran Wrap around the waist" and feel refreshed.

But one day, as I was I lounging in the hospital corridor on a gurney waiting for something or other, a lovely woman resident by the name of Veronica stopped by and we started talking. As I look back, this happened a lot, the random conversations with doctors, nurses, technicians of all kinds. It was interesting and stimulating, getting to know so many people, even if it was just briefly.

Veronica asked me about my history and everything that had happened. She had already read my chart and was quickly connecting all the dots. I told her I felt like a whiner and a bad sport (because of course it could be so much worse) but I was irritated in so many ways by this setup that ripped, leaked, moved, cause my skin to break out and openly weep despite the tiny new attachment.

"You might not always have it, you know," Veronica told me.

"Have what?" I asked.

"The neph tube. After a while you may not need it."

"How can that be?"

 I was intrigued.

"It [the internal plumbing] can heal eventually."

I was astonished. Could Veronica be right?

Wanting to hug her, I practically jumped off the gurney.

As soon as I could get to a phone I called Dr. Kidney.

"Is it true, that maybe I won't always have the neph tube? That I might be able to get rid of it? I thought it was permanent," I said.

"Well, miracles happen, but I wouldn't count on it. After a while you may find it is second nature," he said.

He didn't ask me who told me, and I didn't offer up the information.

A snitch I was not.

But he couldn't take away the nugget of hope that Veronica had given me. I had been daydreaming of being able to travel again, but didn't know how I could possibly manage it.

OK, that is a lie. I wanted to go back to Ireland. I had been looking for any way I could travel with the nephrostomy tube. I thought I may have found a way to avoid a nighttime anti-social mishap. Online there was a collapsible dog bowl where I could park the receptacle by my bed while I slept. That would take care of about 25 percent of the problem.

The big concern was a much bigger one than taking dog bowls to Ireland.

My daughter's wedding was coming up.

For the past two years, every time she came home to New England from the West Coast, even if I was doing OK when we arranged it, I was medically compromised in some way when we got together. No details needed here.

I tried to be positive but I felt vulnerable, pathetic, a loser. Aside from the emotions of my only daughter getting married, the prospect of some sort of hideous malfunction at the rehearsal dinner or on her big day made me break into a sweat.

The worries were reality-based. Eighteen months after the Whipple there was still a very good chance something would go awry.

In the bigger picture, Veronica gave me a gift that day in the hospital corridor. Even if I didn't get rid of the neph tube in time for the wedding, maybe, just maybe, it would happen.

And, a moment of grace did occur.

A couple of weeks before the wedding, after an ultra-sound, Dr. Kidney gave me permission to clamp off the neph tube (which is where the stopcock comes in). If the ureter could function without assistance for two weeks, Dr. Kidney said the tube could be removed.

My system was able to act normal for 10 days, but couldn't go the distance. I was disappointed, but hopeful.

I was one large step closer to the miracle.

36

Mother of the bride

Recovery from cancer surgery didn't turn out to be a linear process like unraveling a sweater. It was more of a rollercoaster of getting better and then things going south and, if you're lucky, recovering to get better again.

I tried to be philosophical about it. Things don't always go wrong, sometimes they go differently. It helps to be flexible in mind as well as body, better to bend than break. The willow and not the oak. Many times it was almost impossible to maintain this attitude, but the more flexible the better. Expectations are everything.

But I had a big-deal event coming up, and I couldn't even take a proper bath. Frustrating. The Saran Wrap didn't stay put; I gave up showers. Too hard, too much of a risk of failure resulting in infection. I got pretty good at the intense sponge bath.

Just four days before the wedding, there was another visit to interventional radiology. Short of convincing them to remove the nephrostomy tube altogether, I asked if there was a special short tube because I was going to a wedding, and not just any old wedding. I was the mother of the star of the show, my firstborn.

The staff rummaged in all the closets for a tube. They tried hard, they were really sweet about it, but eventually gave up. I could have lassoed a calf with the loop of tubing I was toting.

Veronica had given me hope that I was close to being done with all that. Dr. Kidney had given it a shot and promised we would try again in a month or two.

Hard to believe that this day had come. Thirty-one years ago a gaggle of grandmothers, ogling newborns in the hospital nursery, pointed out the child they had elected most beautiful baby. ("Oh, yes, that one's mine. She was born yesterday.") Now she was all grown up and just as beautiful.

Everything about the wedding was gorgeous and elegant, and I couldn't have been happier about the marriage itself. My 6'4" son, brother of the bride, handsome in his tux, walked me down the aisle, then sat down beside me in the first row on the bride's side.

As for me, I loved what I was wearing, but didn't know if I was going to be able corral the yards of tubing into a place where it wouldn't peek out from under the hem of my knee-length dress. A malfunction could have gotten me cut out of the wedding pictures, and that would have been the least of it.

That morning it rained. Good, I thought, get it out of your system. The bride, bridesmaids and I all got our hair and makeup done. I went out for sandwiches and we had lunch with champagne at a friend's house near the hairdresser.

By afternoon the sun came out and the blue sky was dotted with clouds. The wedding was in and around a Victorian house near the Charles River. The flowers were amazing, heavy on hydrangeas, with pale roses and clematis in the bride's bouquet.

Chairs were set up for the ceremony which was to be late afternoon under the arbor in a large garden walled with high hedges.

While the bridesmaids were getting ready upstairs in the bride's room, I found a large bathroom in a far-off corner of the house where I could compose myself. I wound and wound the tubing carefully under the wrap portion of the bodice, then used pins and tape to hold everything together and attached the bag. Bending or kneeling would have been impossible; luckily, it wasn't a Catholic ceremony.

Over the tube I layered everything else: underwear, toeless stockings, Spanx, dress. I gasped; it would be my last deep breath. I was encased in a slightly flowy navy dress with a skirt resembling flower petals, but underneath it was a rock hard, bulletproof suit of spandex, plastic, cloth tape that would tear my skin off and great big diaper pins with yellow duckies on them. I couldn't inhale but the look was amazing.

Next came the earrings, pearl bracelet, and a wonderful necklace of titanium wire hydrangea petals.

The cell phone rang as I was arranging a lavender pashmina shawl. The bride was requesting my presence in her dressing area. Her dress was gorgeous and she would be too; I could not wait to see her.

I sprayed on my sixth or seventh shot of Oscar de La Renta perfume and prayed I wouldn't let this girl of mine down.

Very carefully, I walked up the stairs to join her.

37

Andrea Update: Tubeless

Hi, everybody:

Almost two years to the day I had my first indication of a problem with my kidney, I am tube-free, stopcock free, free to take a bath. I thank every one of you for getting me through the tough times and the tedious times and keeping me laughing at all the things no one else would find funny.

I wore neon orange and black striped Halloween tights into interventional radiology today to get the nephrostomy tube removed.

They are now my lucky tights. I may even wear them on my next flight to Ireland.

Love,

Andrea

Afterword & Acknowledgments

It has been five years since that Friday night I felt the stabbing pain that signaled my kidney was in crisis; four and a half years since the Whipple procedure and three years that I have been free of all physical interventions

Today I am fine, fatter and sassier than I was three years ago. I have follow-up scans for cancer every six months, and so far they have been normal. It is a cause for celebration every single day. I can't say enough good things about my doctors, hospital staff, and my oncology social workers.

Mine is a mild cancer story compared to many. My primary care doctor says that she is amazed that I "keep chugging along on that little piece of kidney that's left." Good health is fragile.

My heart breaks over this rampant disease that affects and ends so many lives. At this stage in life it seems there is always someone close to me in trouble, and I have to remember that I can keep them in my heart long after they are gone. My Irish friend Francis and I had just started corresponding after a long pause when, sadly, he died of cancer himself this past year.

There have been four trips to Ireland since this story ended at my daughter's wedding. I write "Dispatches From Ireland," for a newspaper in my hometown as well as help clients write memoirs and run writing workshops which are inspiring, enlightening, and, often, have to say, just plain hilarious.

Gratitude goes to my friends, you know who you are. I am so terrified of leaving someone out that I am not listing any individual names.

Much love to Abby, Alex, Nate, Chris, and Kathy, my family. I am so grateful that you are all in my life.

And Cassie, the shaggy blonde dog who shares my house, I forgive you for snarling when I finally came home after all those weeks. I can tell you have long ago forgiven me for leaving.

October 2015

Epilogue

It's hard not to love the Arts & Crafts/Craftsman period of architecture and decoration: think William Morris, Charles Rennie Mackintosh, bungalows, brown shingle houses, square roses, birches and most of all ginkgo leaves.

The contents of my house include ginkgo tile, ginkgo earrings and a lacquered black tray with gold ginkgo leaves from a Frank Lloyd Wright house.

The summer before returning home from Ireland to kidney trouble, I had purchased a small ginkgo tree for my front yard.

It was still in its pot the following spring.

I loved the distinctive fan shape of the leaves and looked forward to the chrome yellow color it would turn in the fall.

Ginkgoes are prehistoric trees, some say the oldest trees in existence today. Ginkgoes survived the bombing of Hiroshima. Not every single Buddhist temple has a ginkgo tree standing nearby, but many of them do.

More than color or leaf shape, the ginkgo is all about the message. Because of its history, the ginkgo is a symbol of hope, of survival. The *ginkgo biloba* extract is used as an herbal supplement to promote brain functioning and slow down memory loss.

The summer after the Whipple, friends did a lot of nice things for me. Marlene was one of them, and she planted the small ginkgo tree in front of my dining room window.

That fall it died.

The following spring it sent up a long side shoot, put out some leaves that yellowed in early August and then that shoot died.

How could the tree not survive? It was peacetime in Massachusetts, expertly planted on a suburban front lawn with water and a little fertilizer and a whole lot of TLC.

The next spring a third shoot appeared, just as strong and tall as the first two. This time it kept going.

Now it has tripled its original height. It will never be the prettiest tree, with its branches sticking out at random angles, but it is thriving. The bright yellow leaves fall off all at once, on single day, but that day is in the autumn, not summer.

This little tree could grow to be 165 feet tall someday.

I won't be around to see it happen, and that's perfectly okay.